I0505605

Brantford Ontario and Area In Colour Photos, Saving Our History One Photo at a Time

Photography
by Barbara Raué
2012

Series Name:
Cruising Ontario

Book 95: Brantford

Cover photo: Brantford House see Page 32

Series Name: Cruising Ontario
Saving Our History One Photo at a Time
in colour photos

Other Books by Barbara Raue

Coins of Gold

Arrows, Indians and Love

The Life and Times of Barbara
Volume 1: Inventions That Have Enhanced My Life
Volume 2: Entertainment That I Have Enjoyed
Volume 3: East Coast Trips
Volume 4: Olympics Have Always Intrigued Me
Volume 5: Wonders of the World
Volume 6: Caribbean Cruises We Have Enjoyed
Volume 7: Animals
Volume 8: Storms and Other Major Disasters in My Lifetime
Volume 9: Wars, Terrorist Attacks and Major Disasters

The Cromwell Family Book

Laura Secord Discovered

Visit Barbara's website to view all of her books
http://barbararaue.ca

Brantford

Brantford is a city located on the Grand River in Southern Ontario. Brantford is connected to Woodstock in the west and Hamilton in the east by Highway 403 and to Cambridge to the north and Simcoe to the south by Highway 24. Brantford is known by the nickname *The Telephone City* as former city resident Alexander Graham Bell conducted the first distant telephone call from the community to Paris, Ontario in 1876. It is also the birthplace of hockey player Wayne Gretzky.

Iroquoian-speaking people lived in the Grand River valley area before the 17th century; their main village and seat of the chief, Kandoucho, was located on the Grand River where present-day Brantford developed.

In 1784, Captain Joseph Brant and the Six Nations Indians of the Iroquois Confederacy left New York State for Canada. As a reward for their loyalty to the British Crown, they were given a large land grant on the Grand River. The original Mohawk settlement was on the south edge of the present-day city at a location favourable for landing canoes. Brant's crossing of the river gave the original name to the area: Brant's ford. By 1847, European settlers began to settle further up the river at a ford in the Grand River and named their village Brantford. Brantford was incorporated as a city in 1877.

Shakespeare

This tiny village located on Highway 7 and 8 between New Hamburg and Stratford was known as Bell's Corners after David Bell who founded the village. In 1852, the name was changed to Shakespeare.

Bethel Road

Bethel Road is located south of Highway 403, northwest of Brantford and south of Paris.

Falkland

Falkland is located on Falkland Road and King Edward Street, west of Paris, southeast of Etonia.

Eastwood

Captain Drew named it Eastwood Park, from which is derived Eastwood Village. Eastwood is west of Woodstock on Dundas Street, and east of Highway 401.

Etonia

Etonia is located on Governors and Canning Roads, north of Highway 403, west of Paris.

Brantford

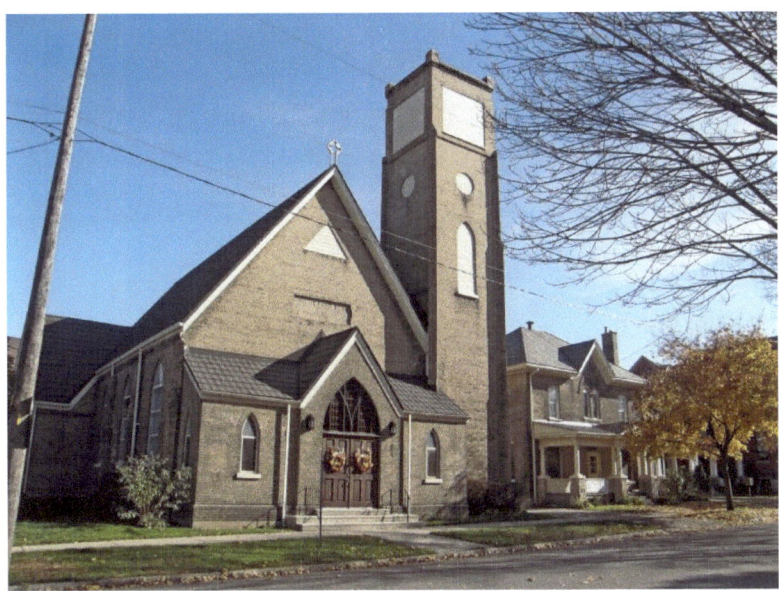

St. Jude's Anglican Church

Table of Contents

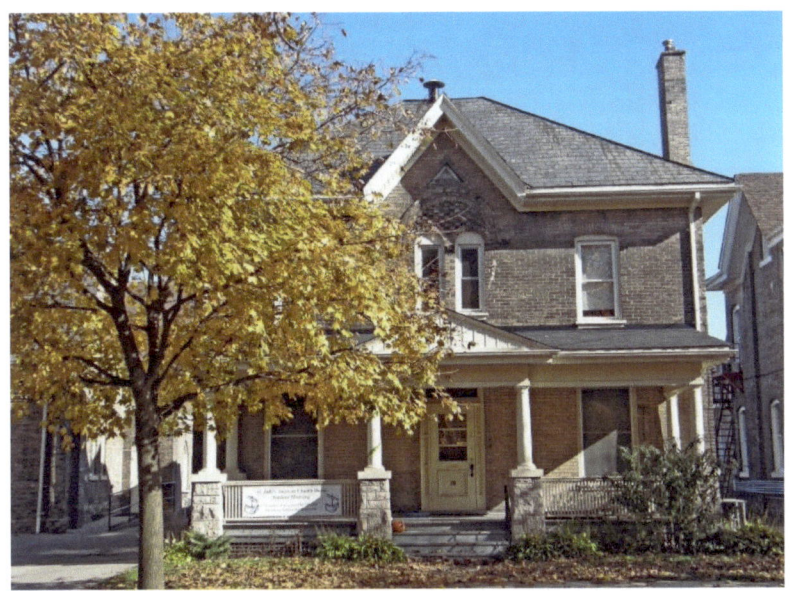

St. Jude's Anglican Church student housing
Centre gable Gothic Revival cottage

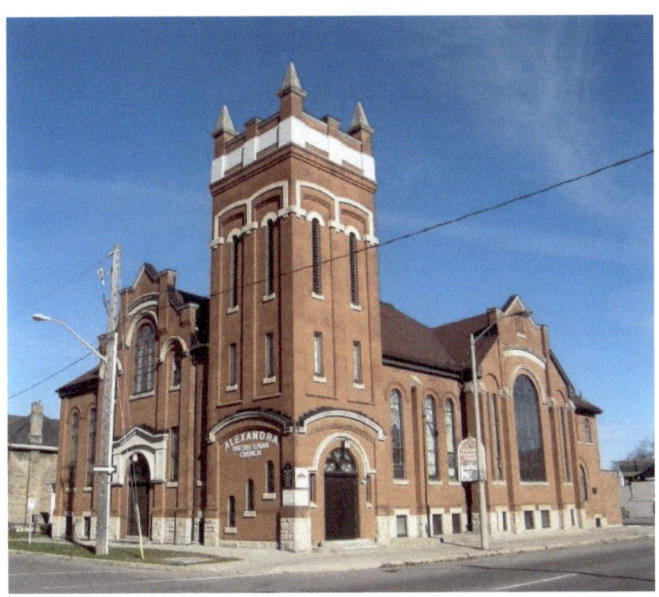

Alexandra Presbyterian Church – 1912

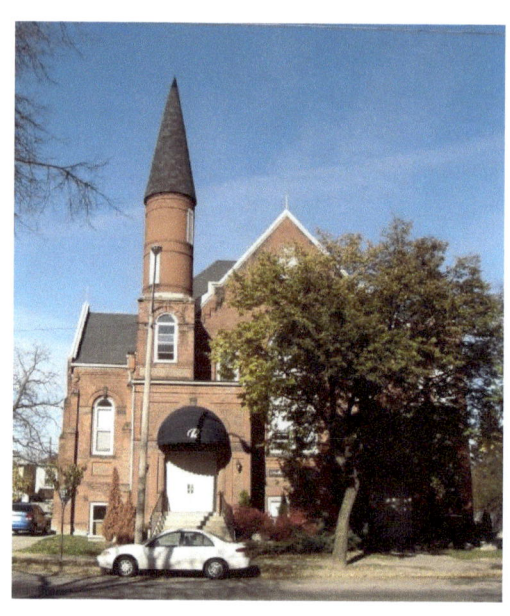

Calvary Baptist Church

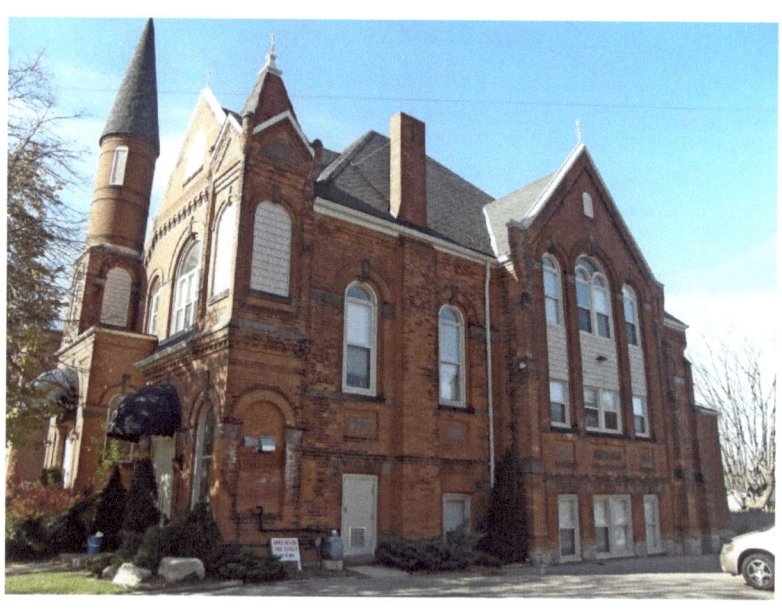

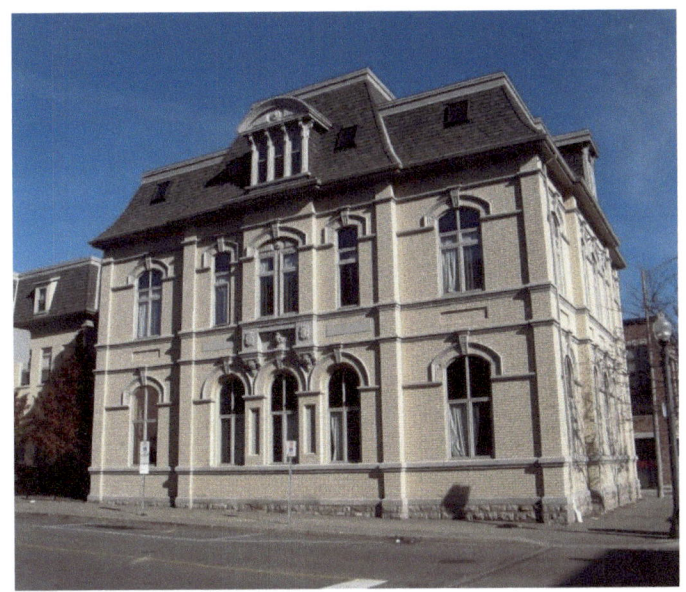

Second Empire – mansard roof, arched voussoirs and keystones

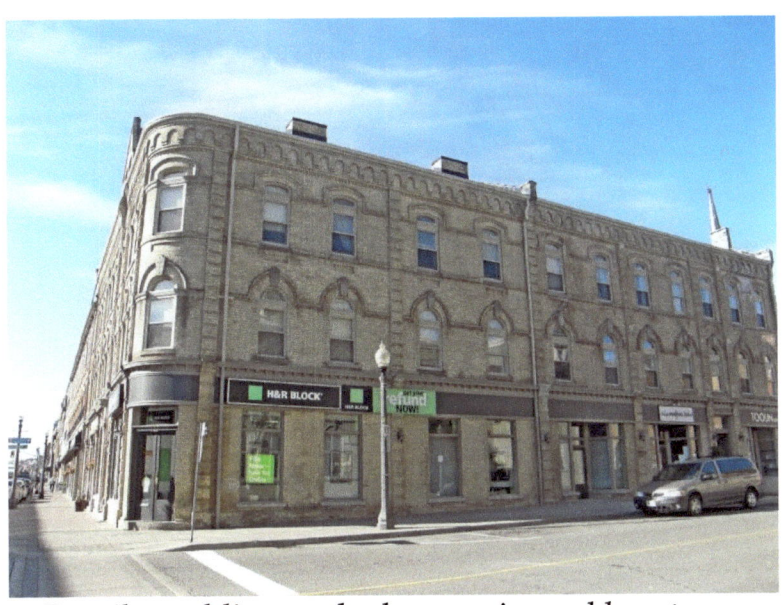

Dentil moulding, arched voussoirs and keystones

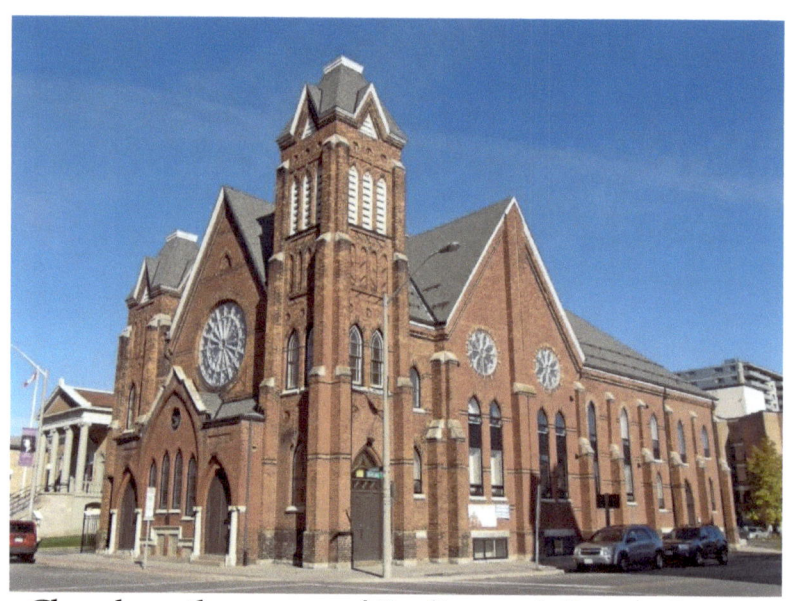

Church on the corner of Darling and George Streets
Built circa 1870 – now student housing
Buttresses, rose windows

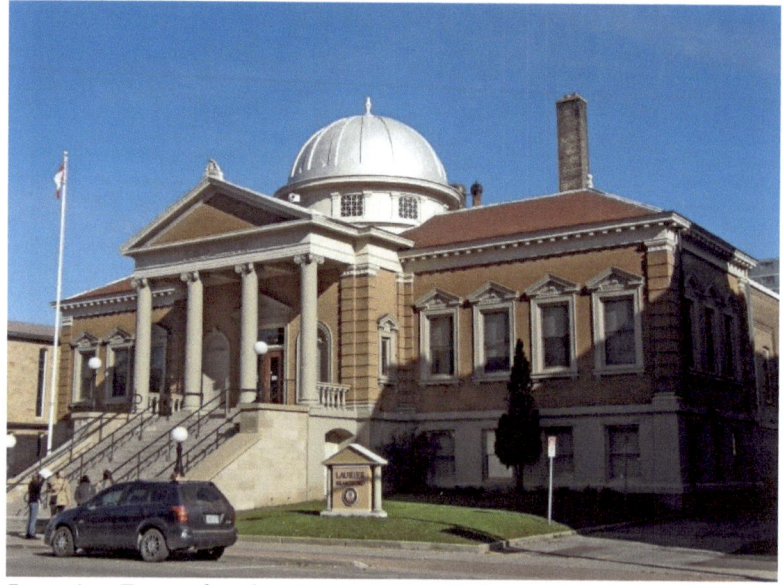

Laurier Brantford – Ionic capitals on pillars, pediment

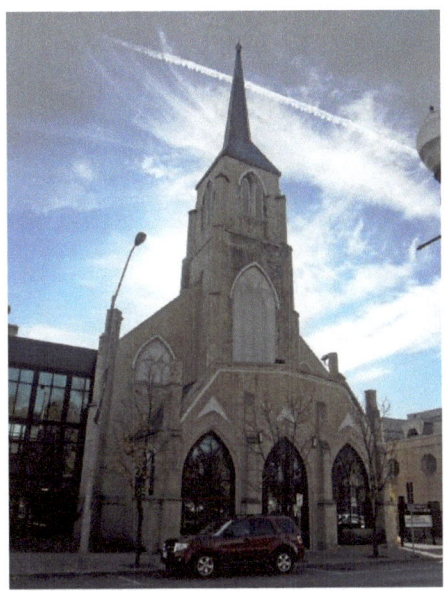

St. Andrews United Church

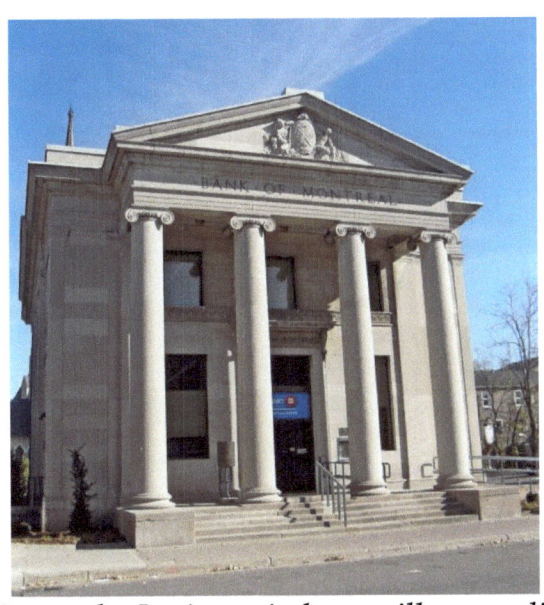

Bank of Montreal – Ionic capitals on pillars, pediment with decorated tympanum

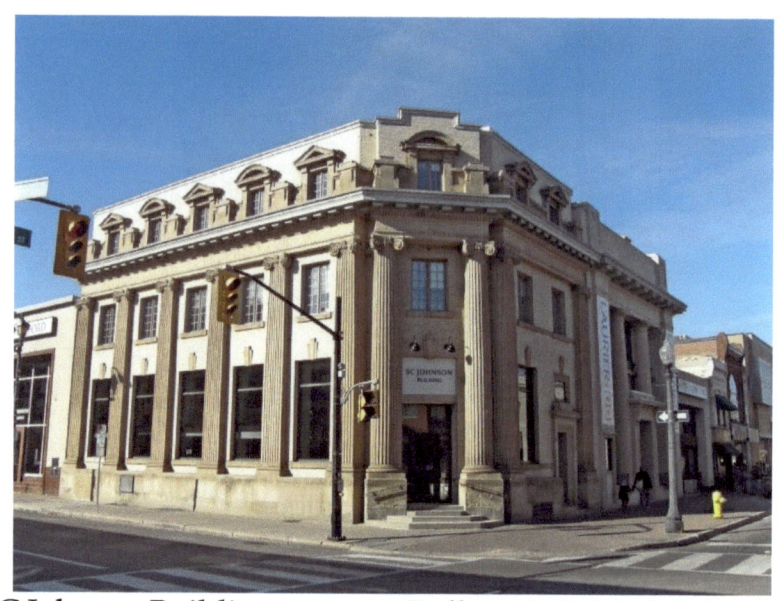

SC Johnson Building – corner Dalhousie & Market Streets,
mansard roof with dormers with triangular window hoods

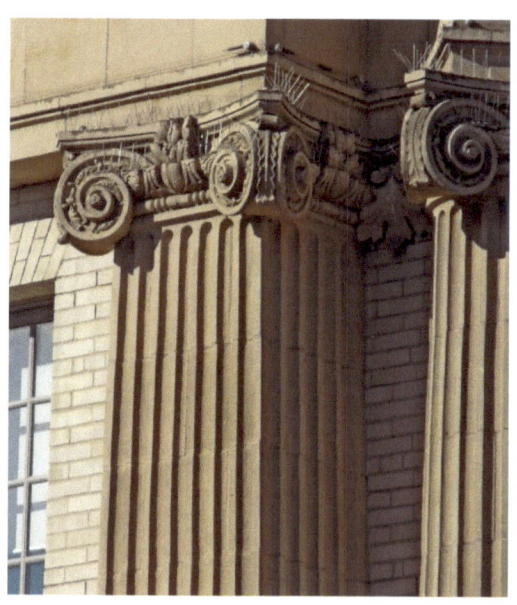

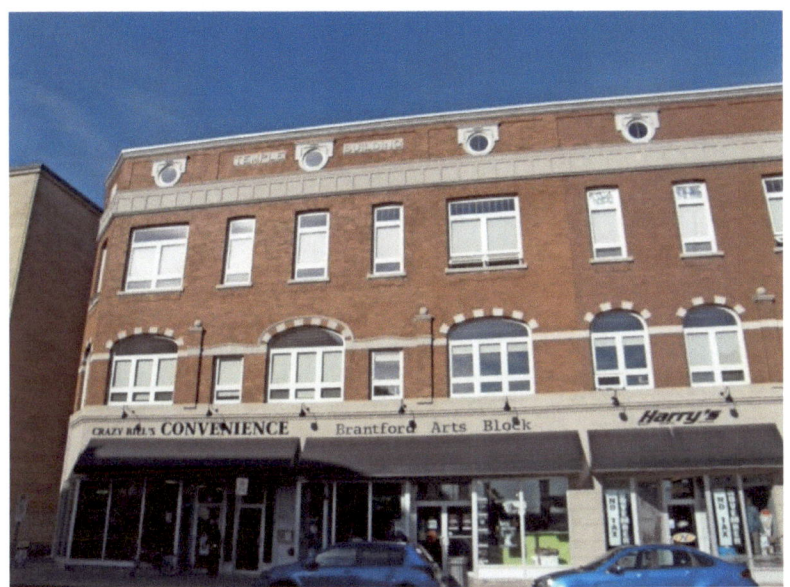

Temple Building – dichromatic window voussoirs

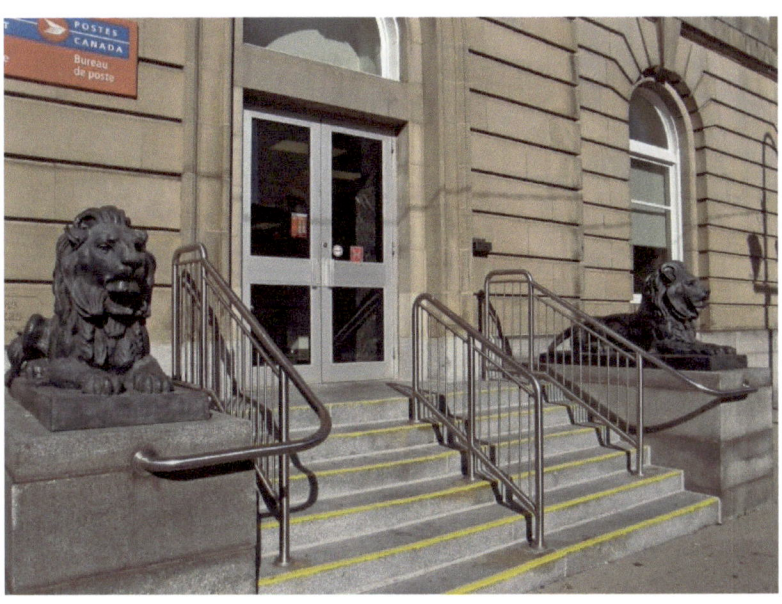

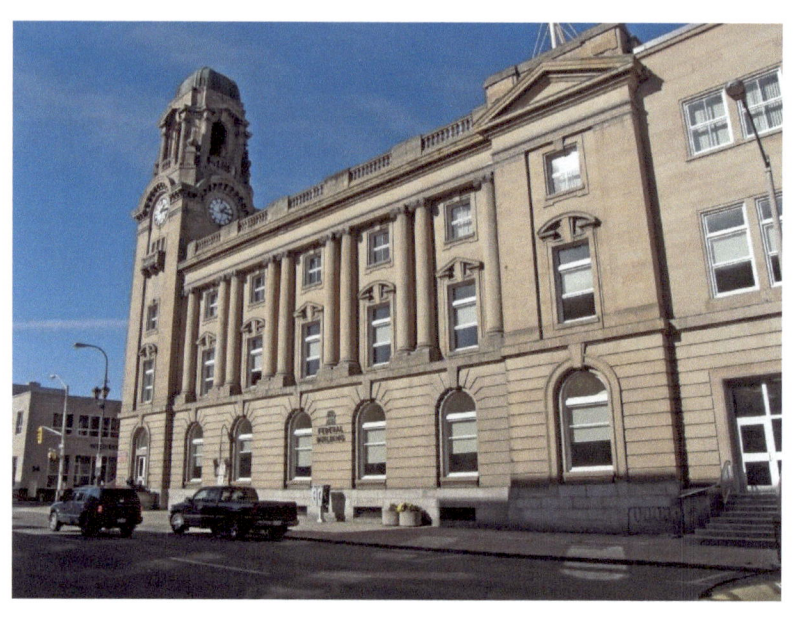

Federal Building – erected 1913 – Beaux Arts style,
pilasters with Ionic capitals

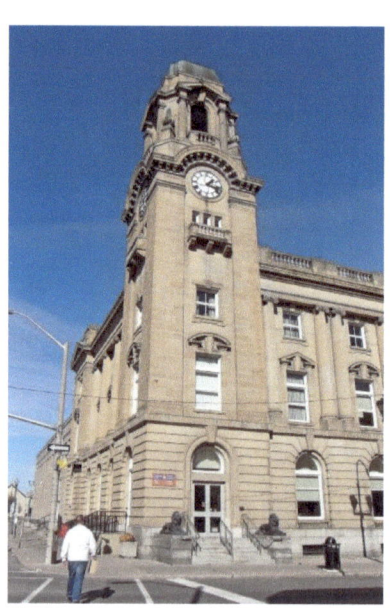

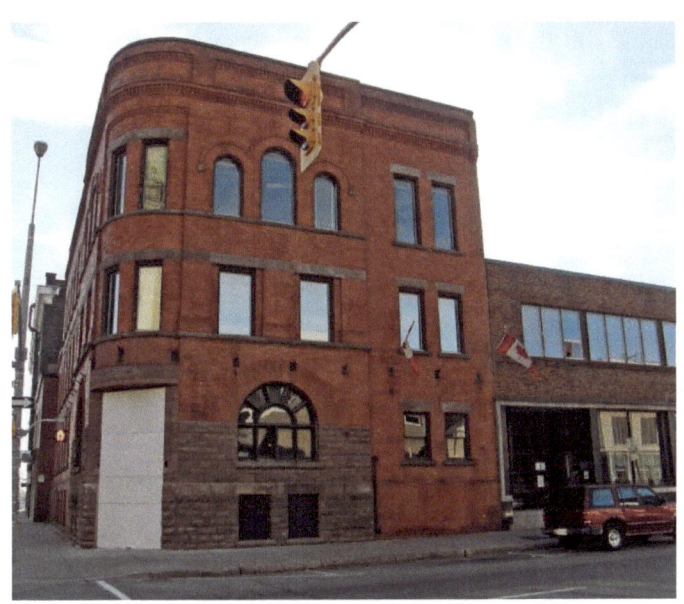

Expositor Building – dentil moulding

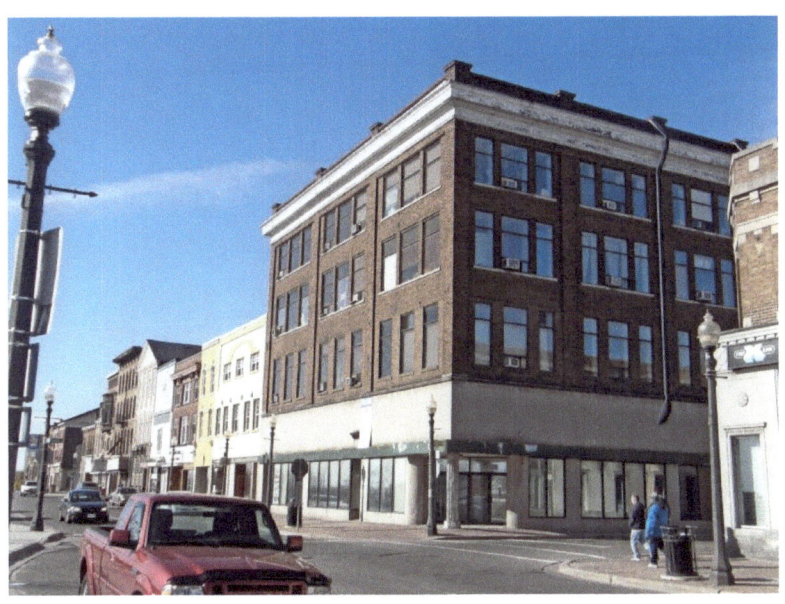

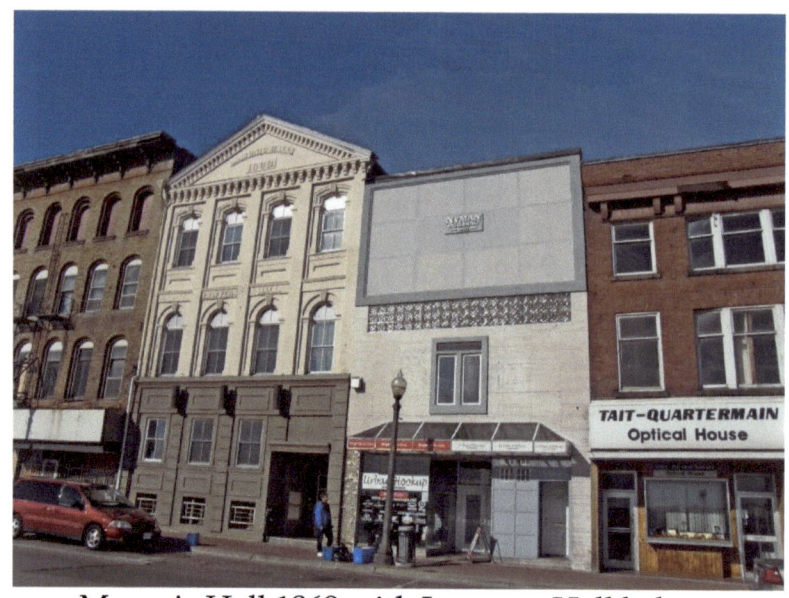

Masonic Hall 1869 with Lawyers Hall below,
Nyman Building to the right - 1897
Cornice brackets, pediment, keystones

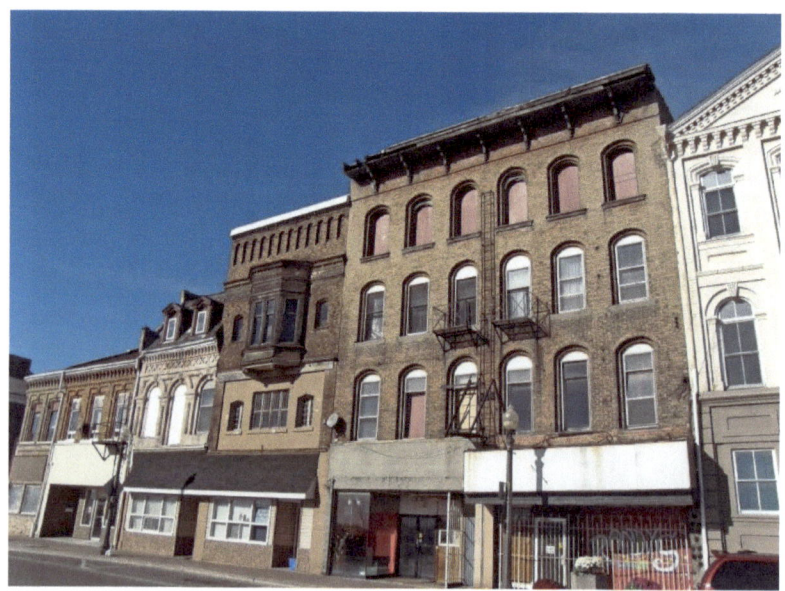

Single cornice brackets, bay window, dormers to left

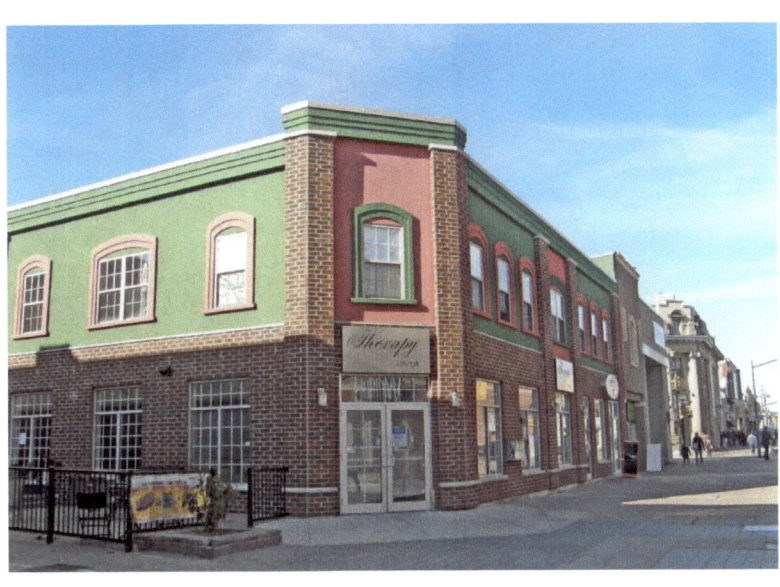

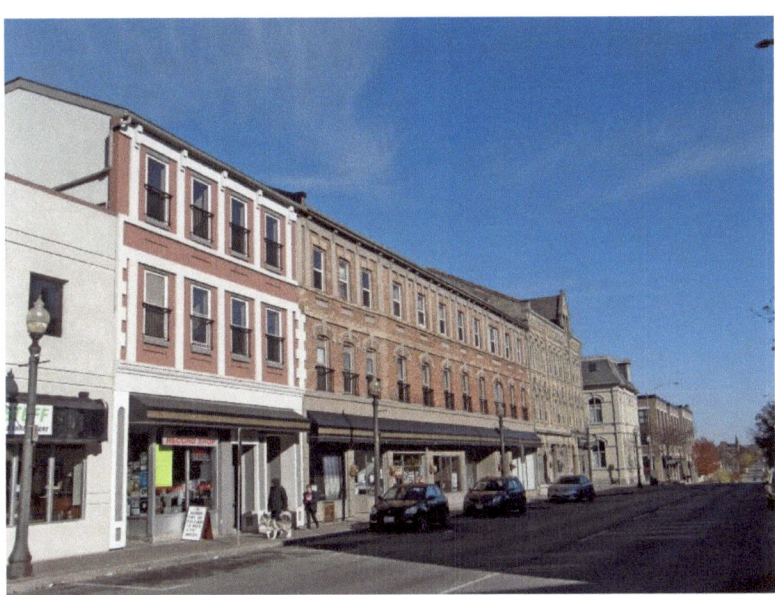

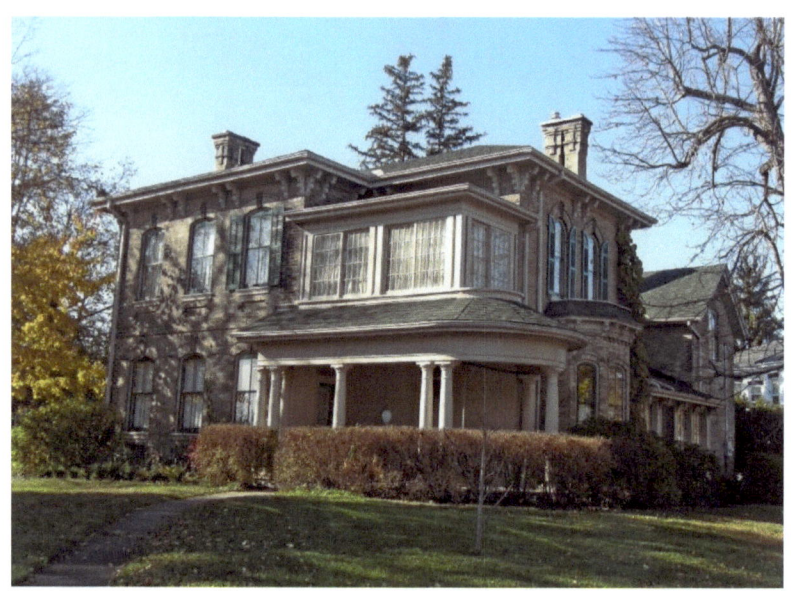

Italianate - paired cornice brackets, Doric pillars
Bay window

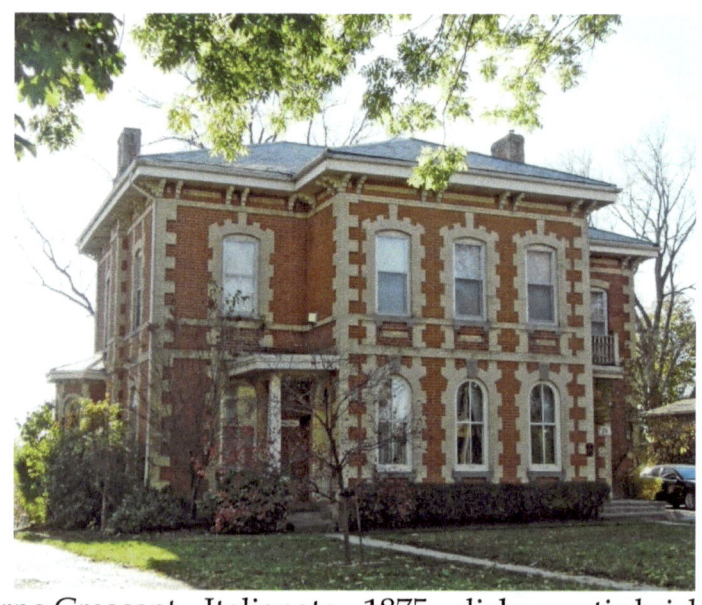

26 Lorne Crescent - Italianate - 1875 - dichromatic brickwork,
paired cornice brackets, bay window on side

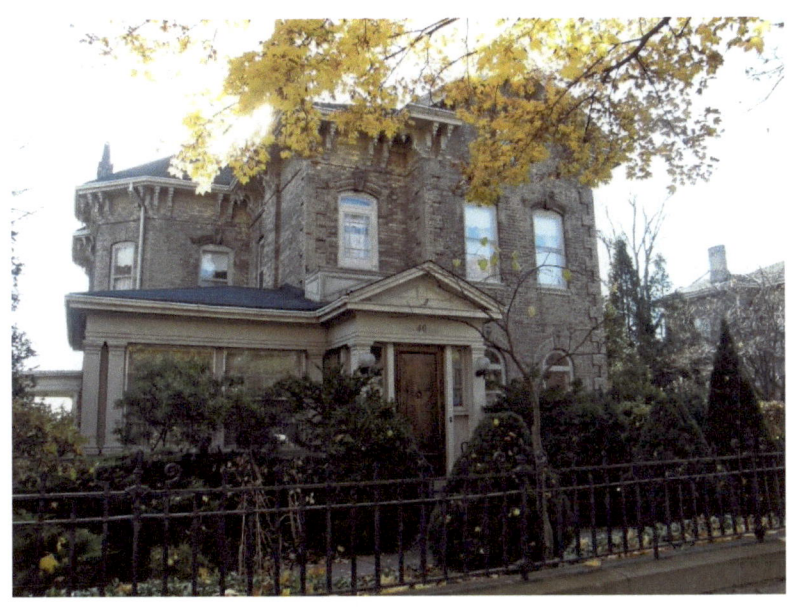

40 Lorne Crescent – 1875 -Gothic Revival - cornice brackets, cornice return on gable

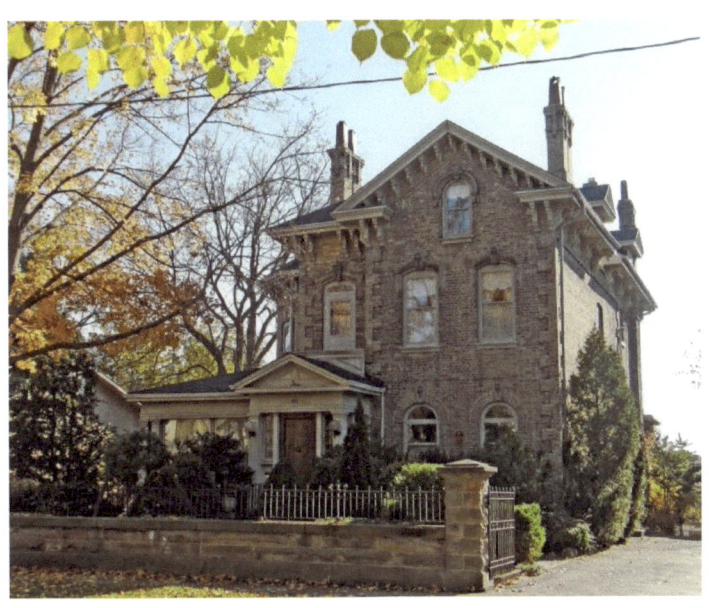

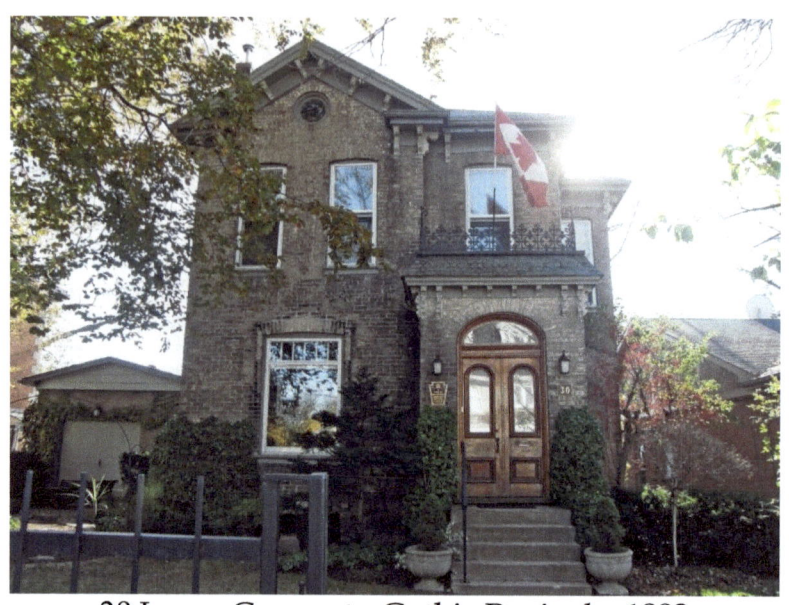

30 Lorne Crescent - Gothic Revival – 1892
single cornice brackets, cornice return on the gable,
iron cresting above entrance

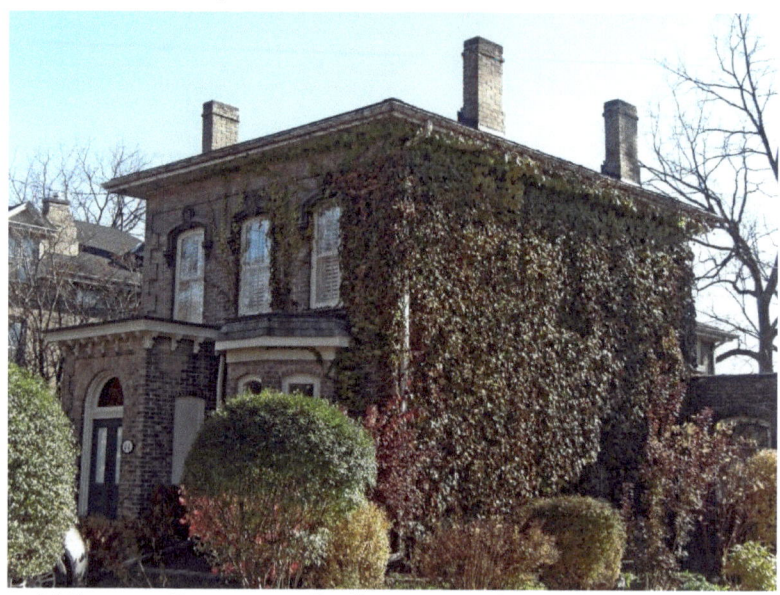

44 Lorne Crescent - Italianate – 1875 – bay window

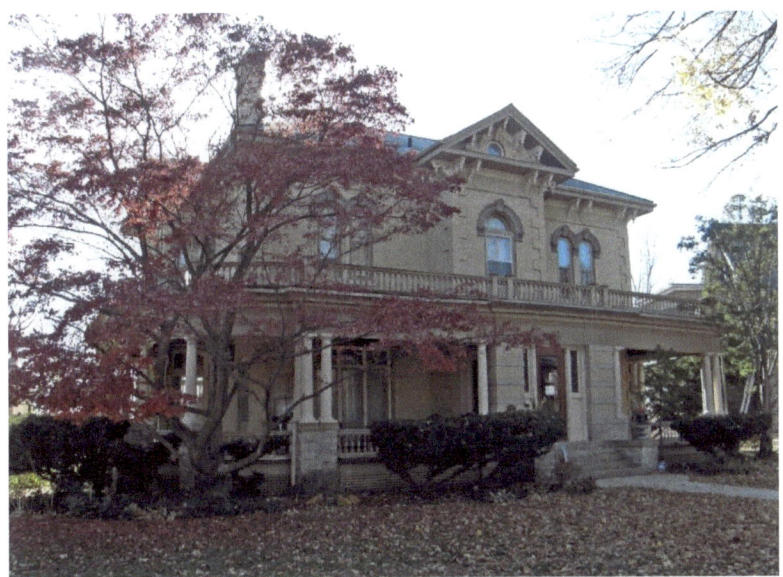

Italianate – 1874 – with 2½ storey frontispiece, cornice brackets, keystones, 1st and 2nd floor wraparound verandahs

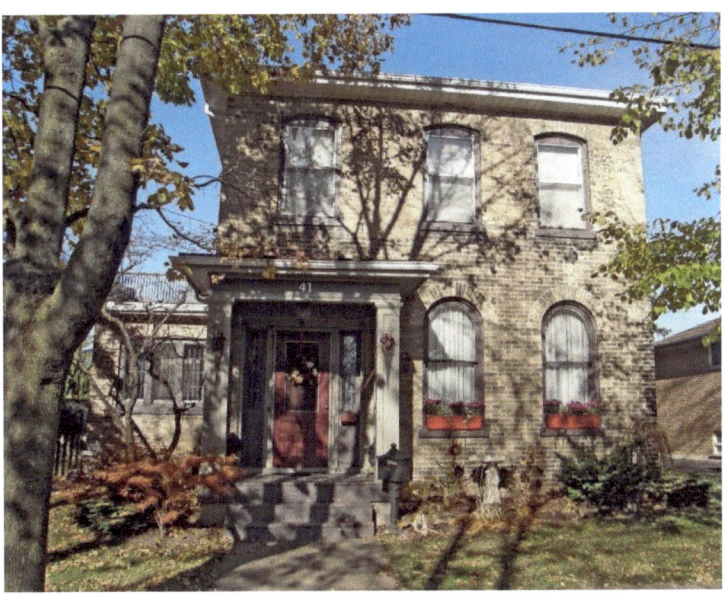

41 Lorne Crescent - Italianate

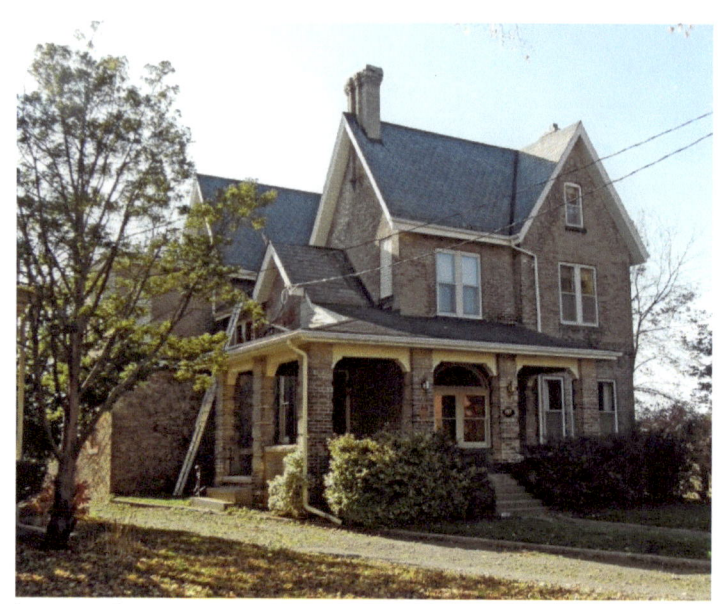

52 Lorne Crescent - 1887 – yellow brick, Gothic Revival

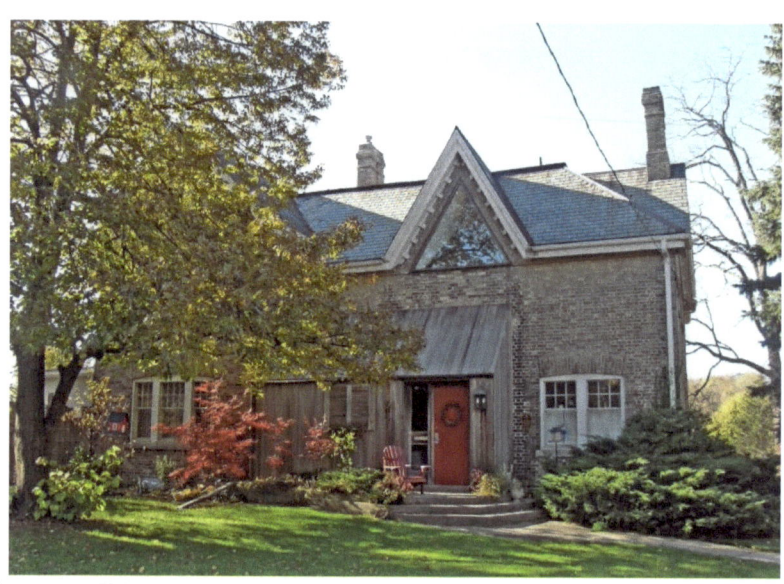

54 Lorne Crescent - 1875 – Gothic Revival

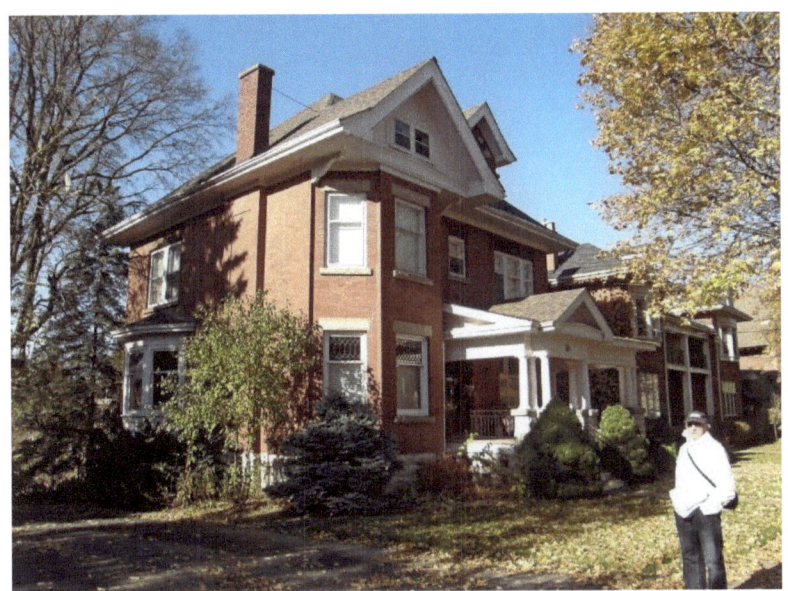

58 Lorne Crescent - 1895 – Edwardian – pediment,
dormer in attic

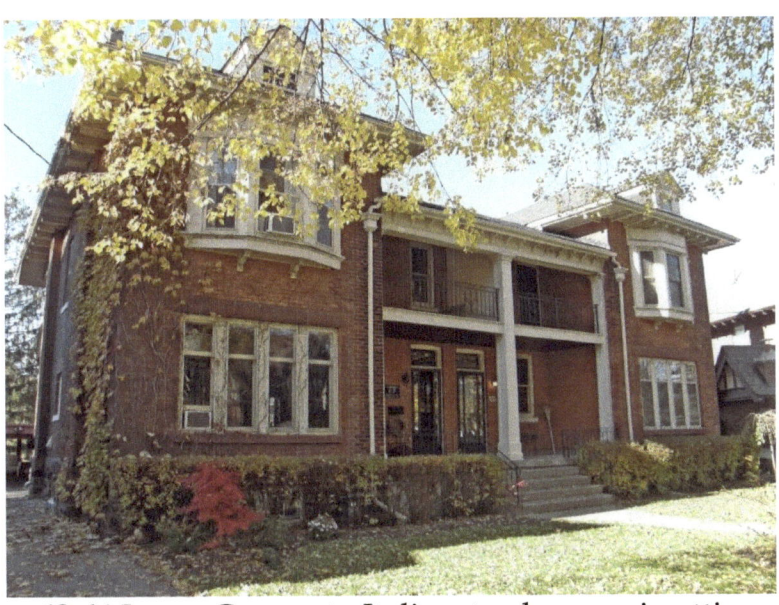

62-64 Lorne Crescent - Italianate, dormers in attic,
second floor bay windows

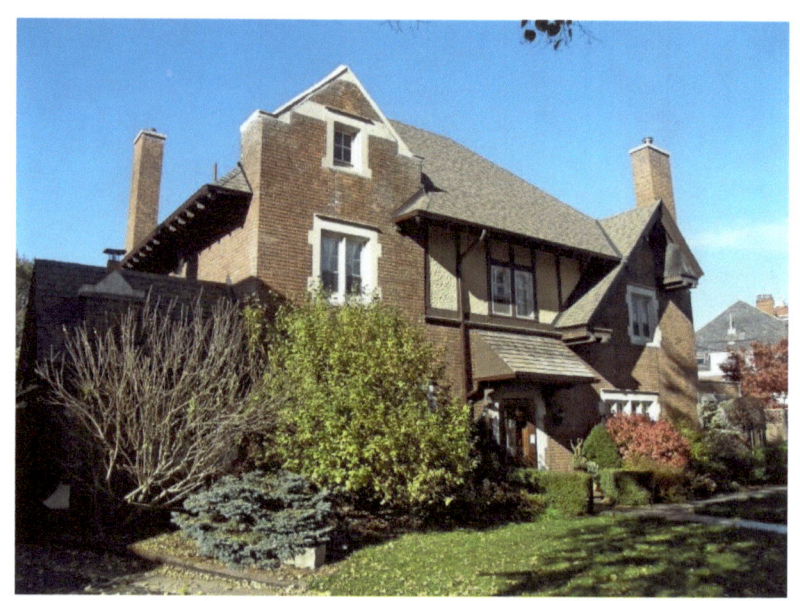

Brick with Tudor accents on plaster

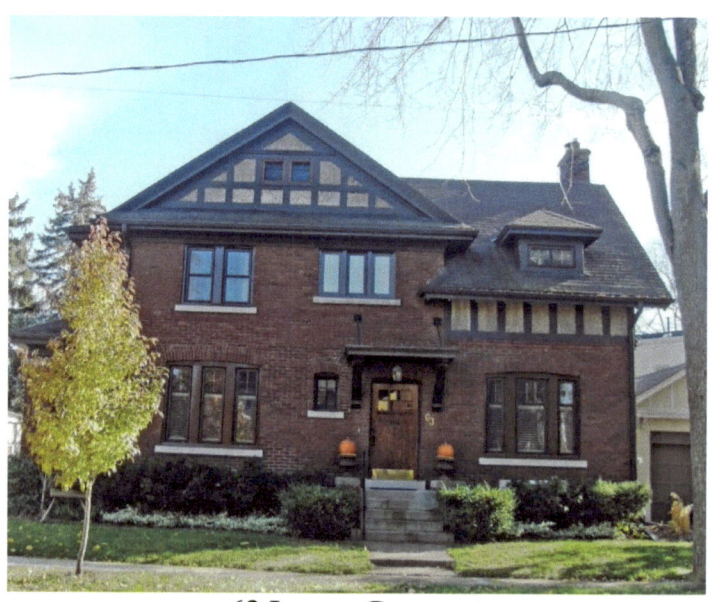

63 Lorne Crescent

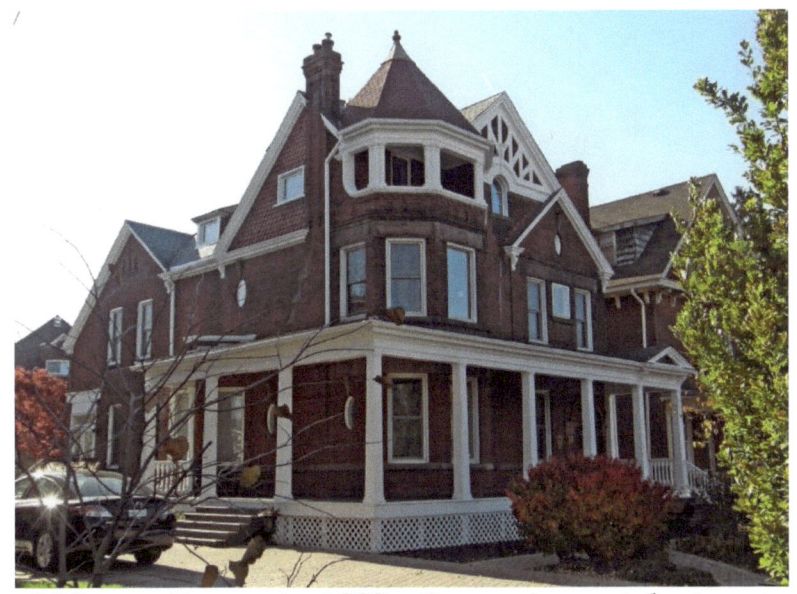

38 Lorne Crescent – 1898 – Queen Anne style, turret

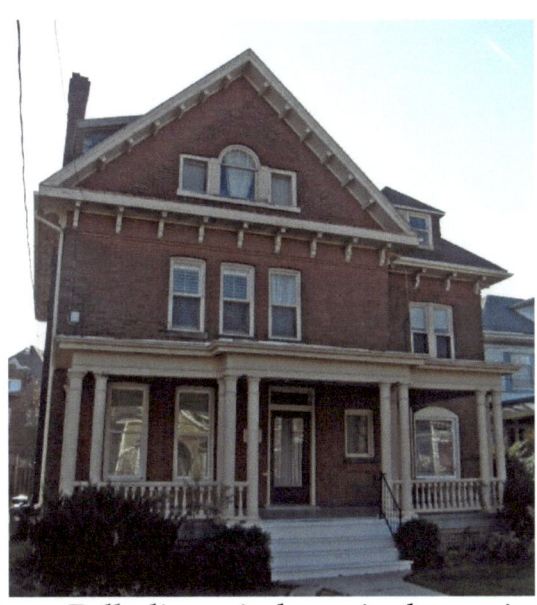

Edwardian – Palladian window, single cornice brackets

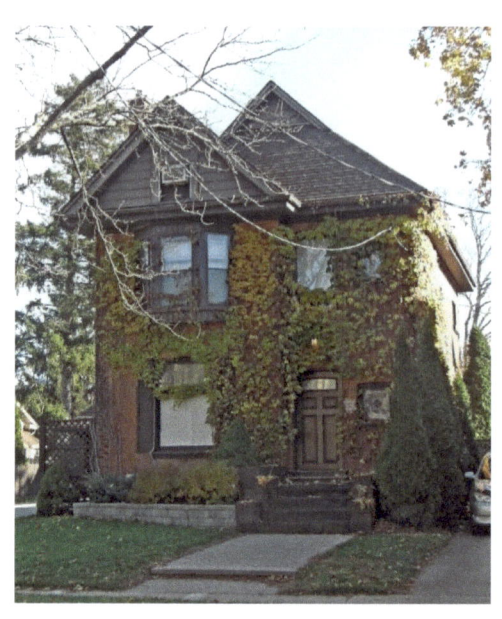

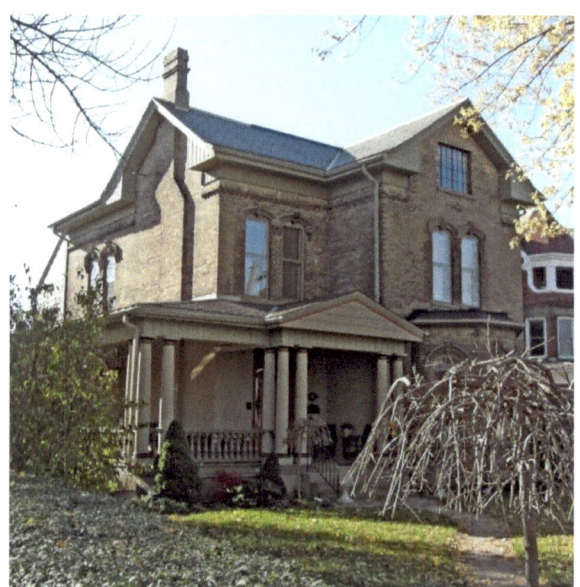

12 Lorne Crescent – Gothic Revival, pediment

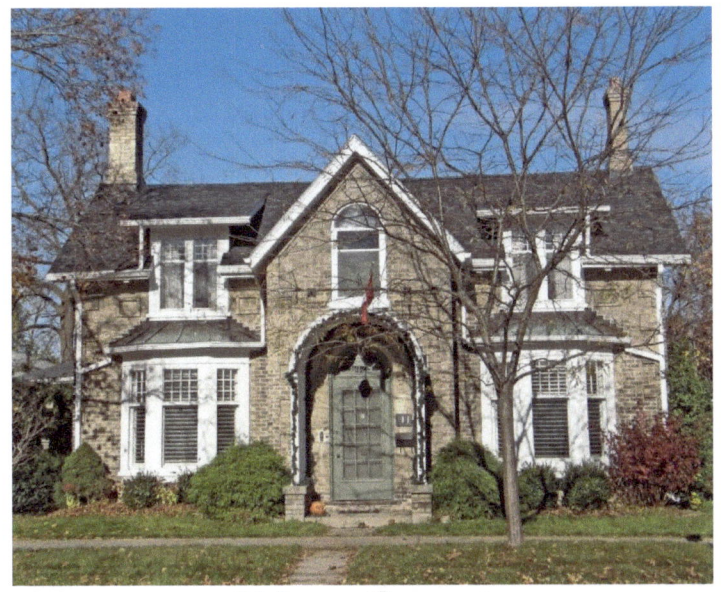

11 Lorne Crescent

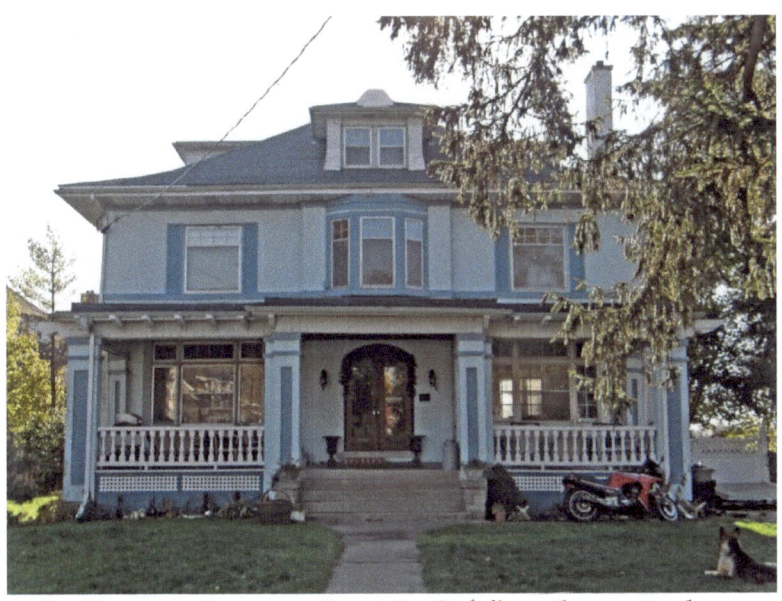

Italianate, dormers in attic, 2nd floor bay window

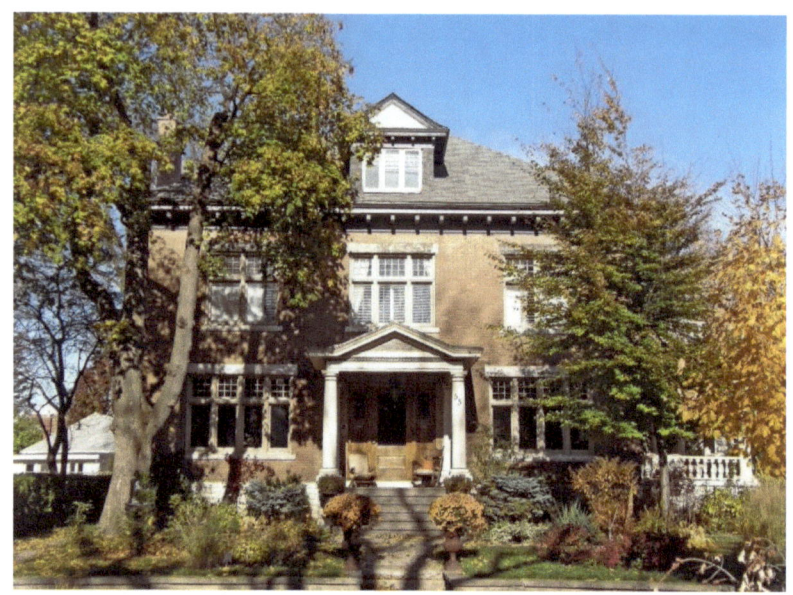

#55 - Italianate, dormer in attic, pediment

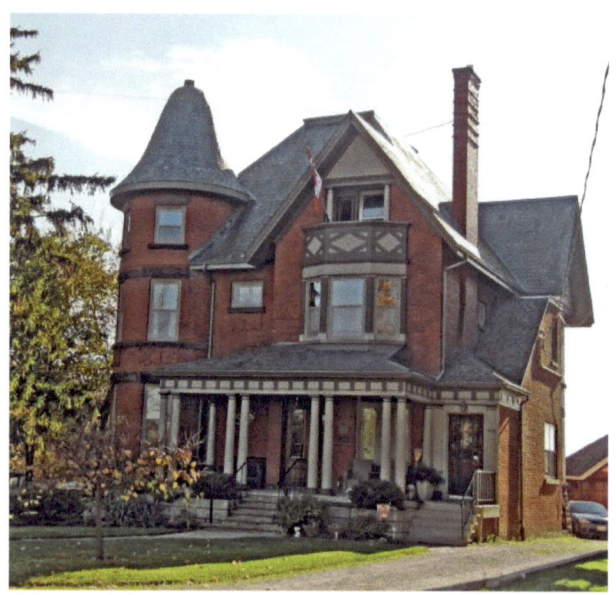

#30 - 1896 – Queen Anne style - round turret

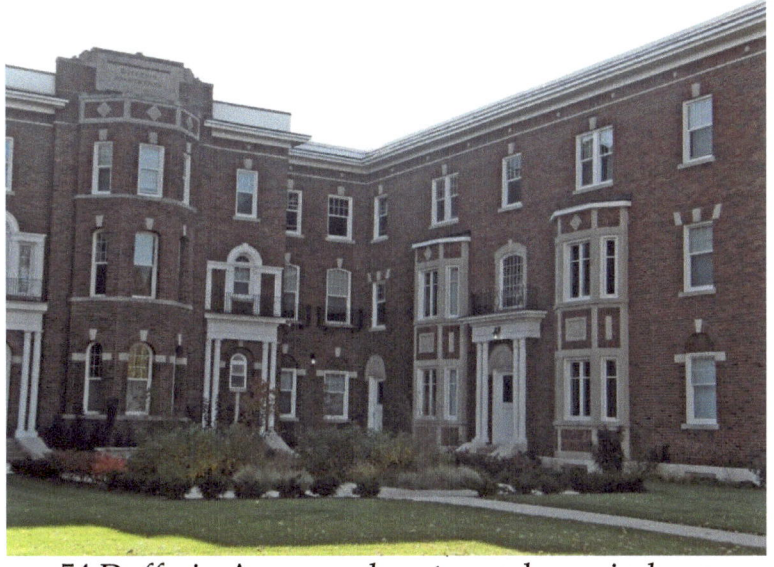

54 Dufferin Avenue – keystones, bay windows

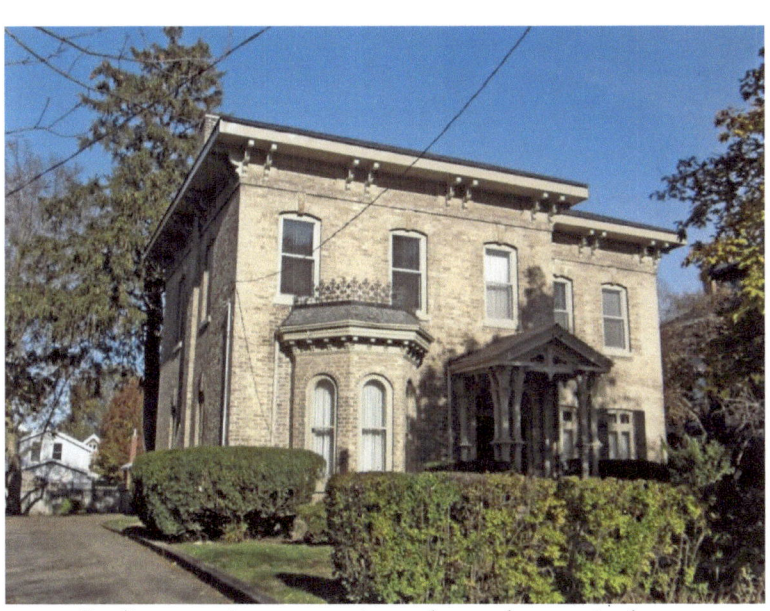

Italianate, iron cresting above bay window,
paired cornice brackets

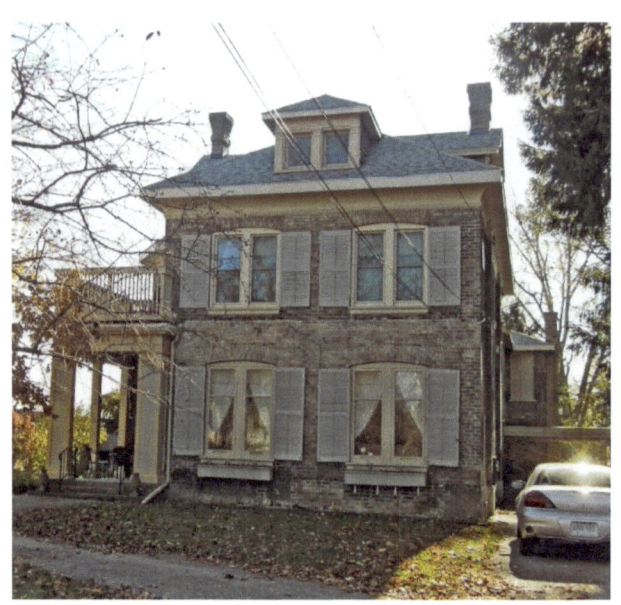

Italianate, dormer in hipped roof

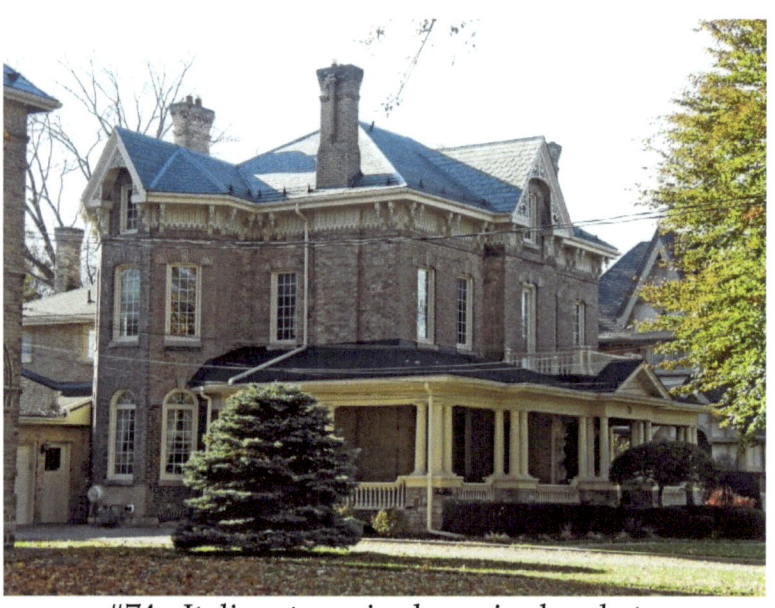

#74 - Italianate, paired cornice brackets,
gingerbread trim on gables

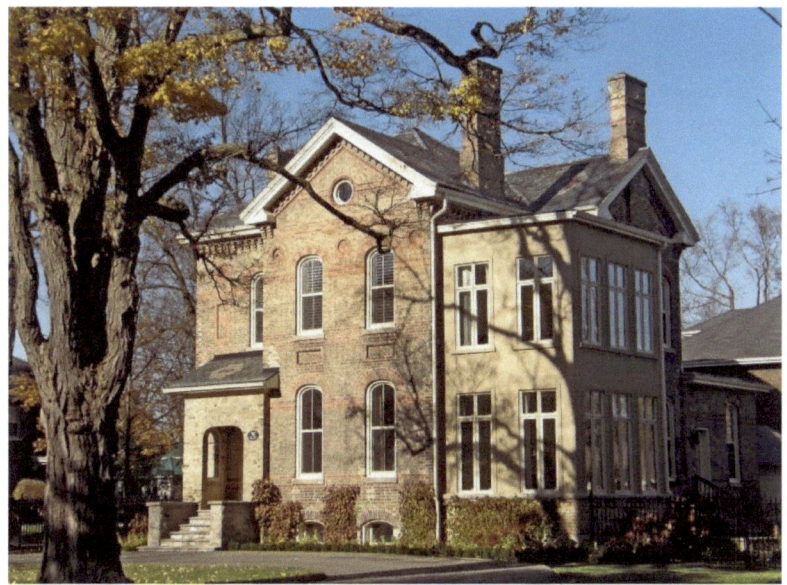

#75 - cornice return and dentil detailing, banding, dichromatic brickwork, polychromatic tile work on roof

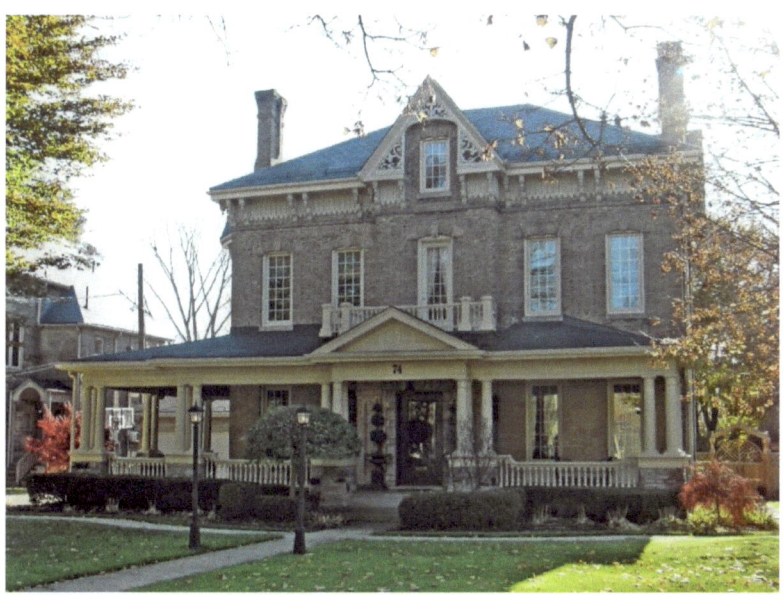

#74 – Italianate with 2½ storey frontispiece, wraparound verandah, pediment, second floor balcony, verge board

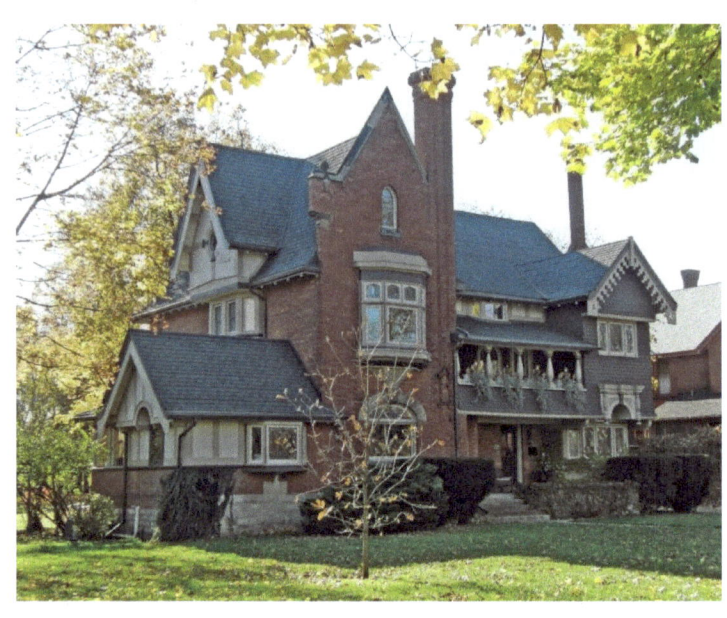

Gothic – verge board trim with finial, Tudor accents on end gables, bay window and balcony on second floor

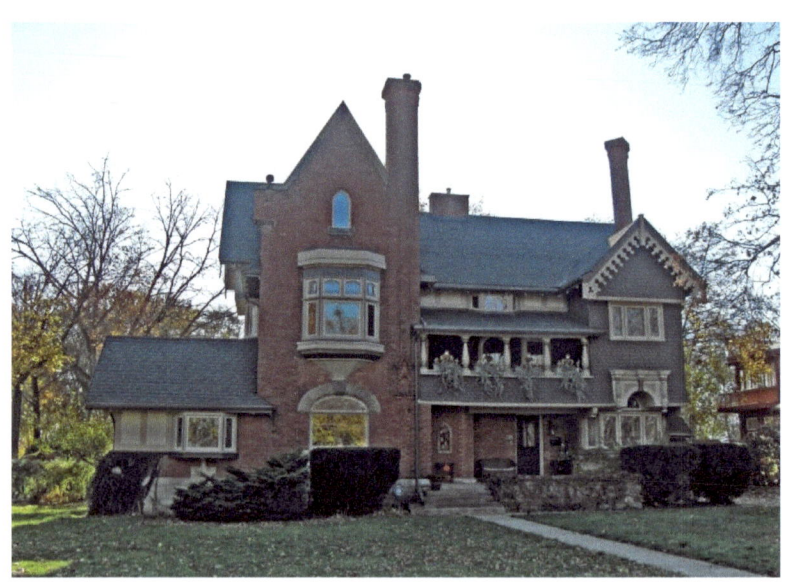

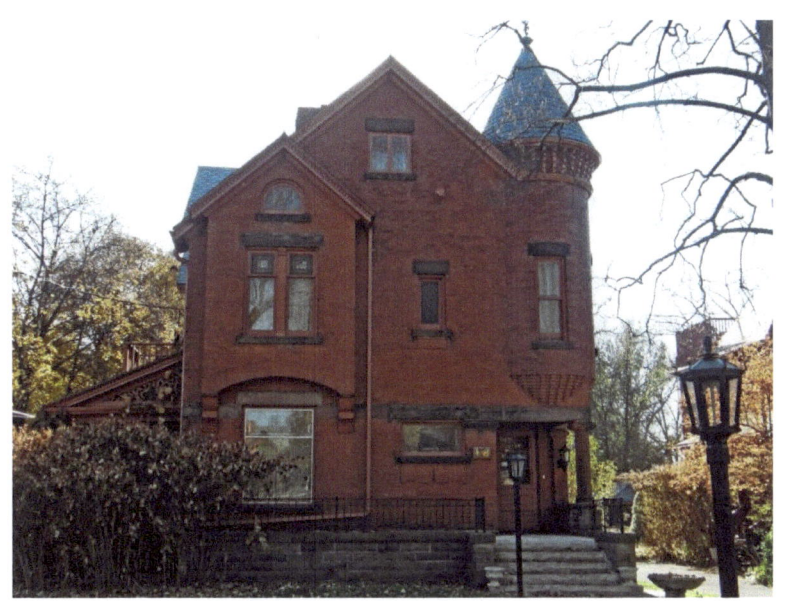

Queen Anne style, turret

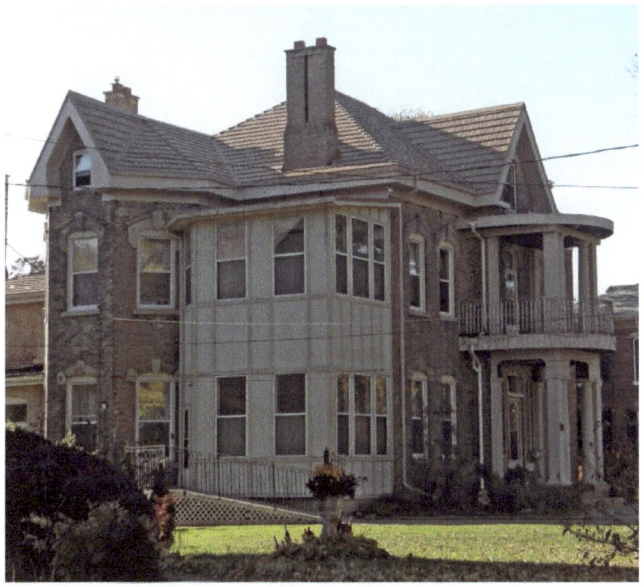

Yellow brick, Gothic Revival,
semi-circular balcony on second floor

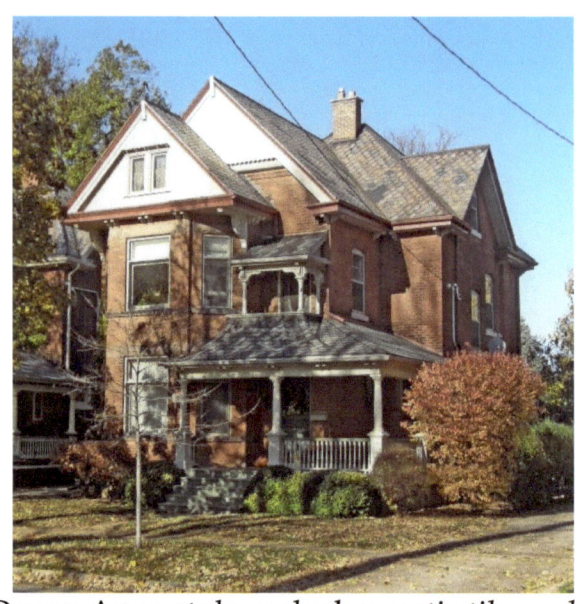

1899 – Queen Anne style, polychromatic tilework on roof

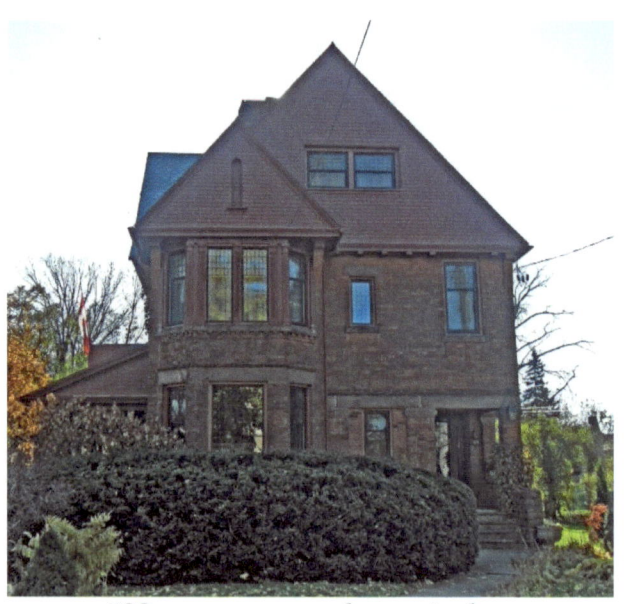

#92 – two-storey bay window

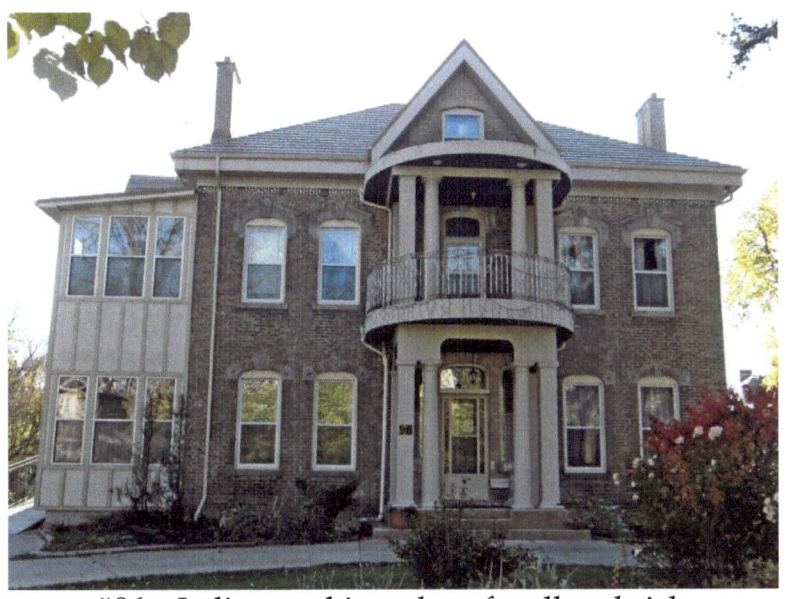

#96 – Italianate, hipped roof, yellow brick,
second floor semi-circular balcony

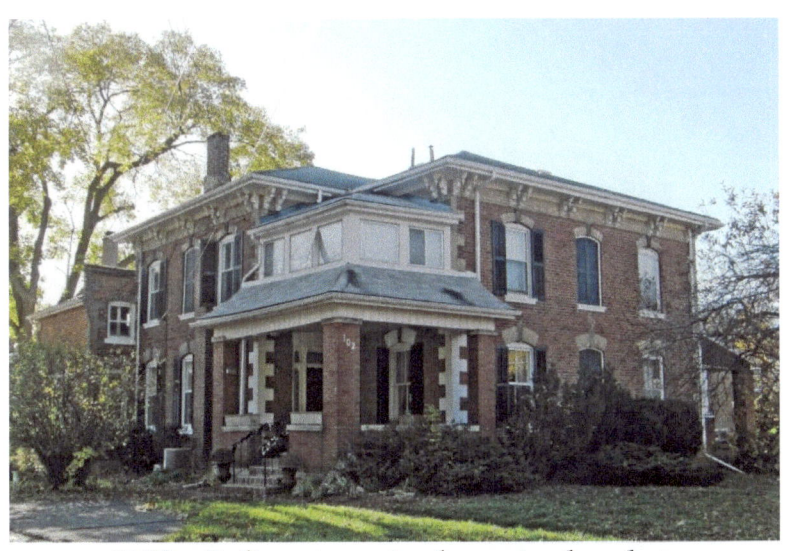

#102 – Italianate, paired cornice brackets

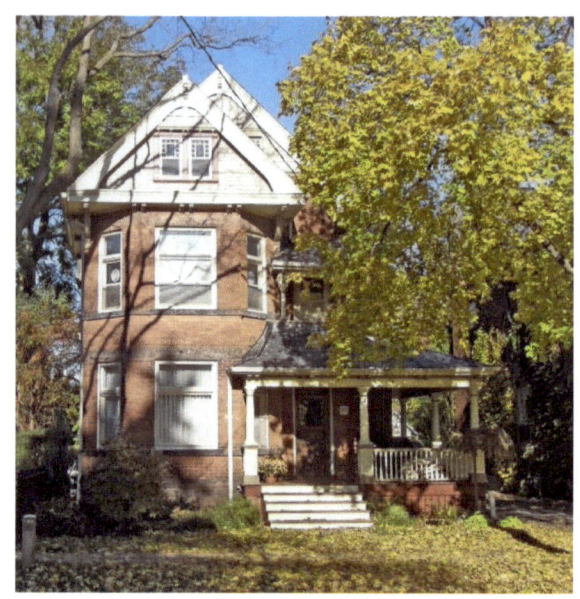

Edwardian

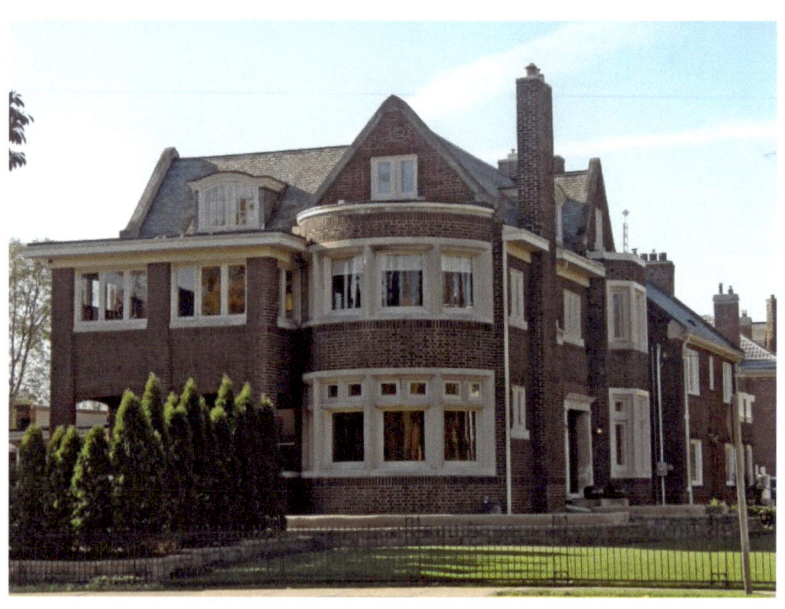

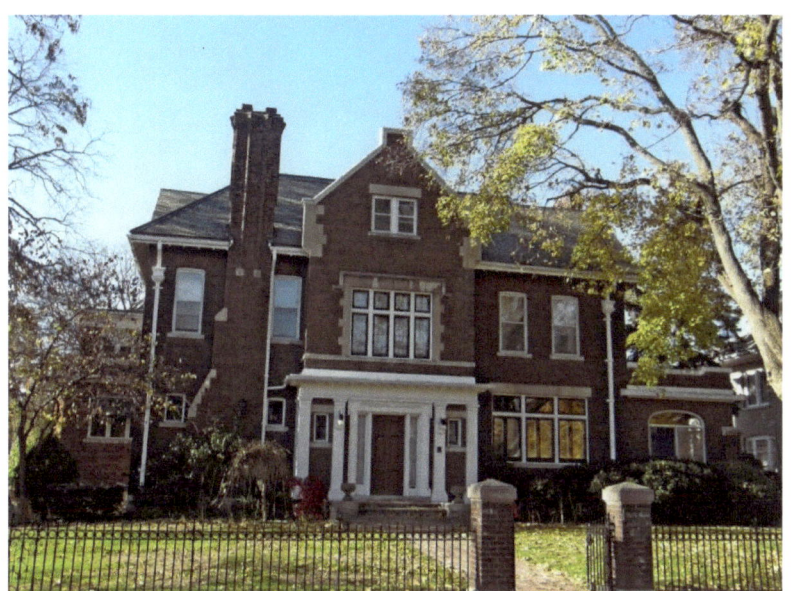

Italianate, 2½ storey frontispiece

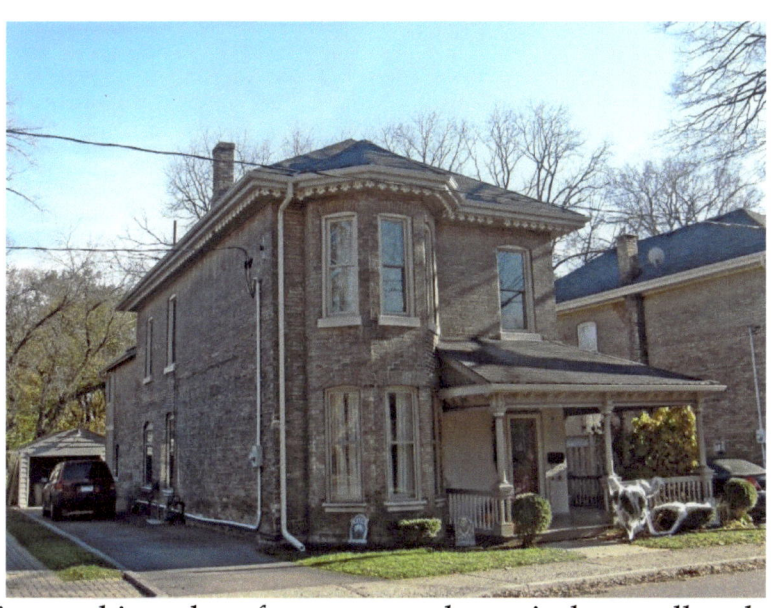

Italianate, hipped roof, two-storey bay window, yellow brick, cornice trim

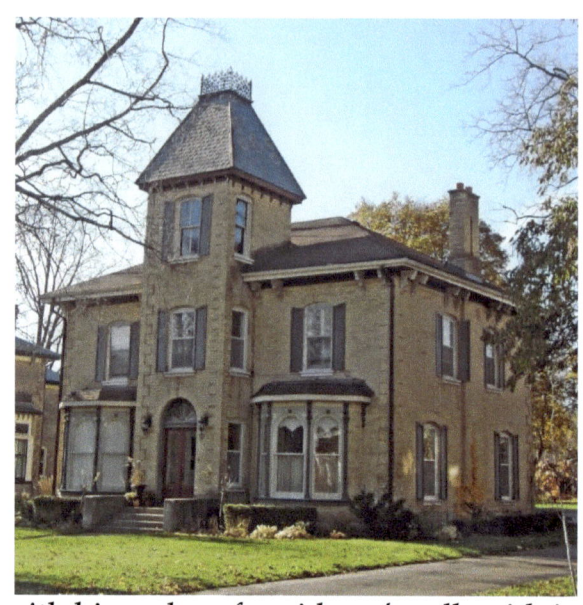

Italianate with hipped roof - widows' walk with iron cresting on the roof of the three-storey tower

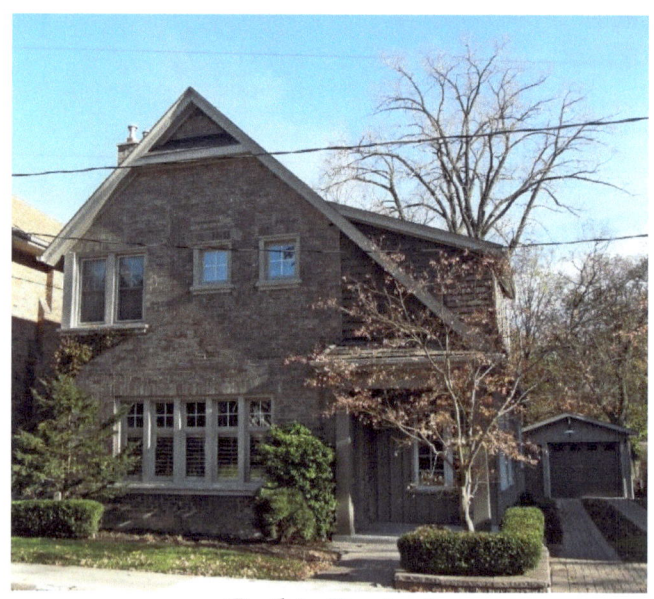

Gothic Revival

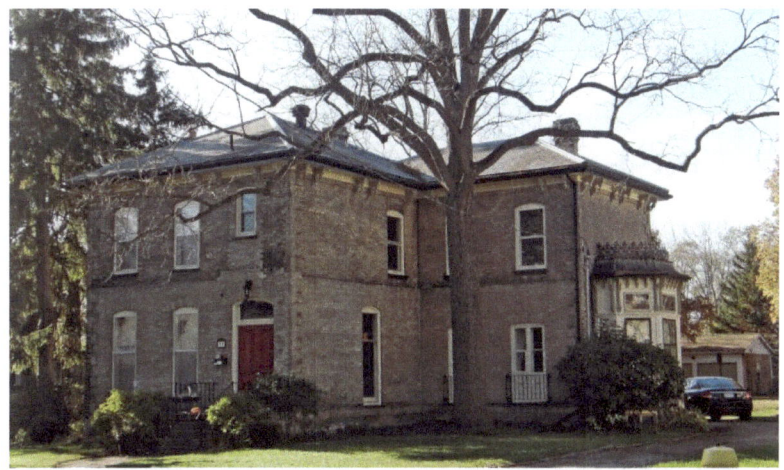

#59 – Italianate, hipped roof, paired cornice brackets

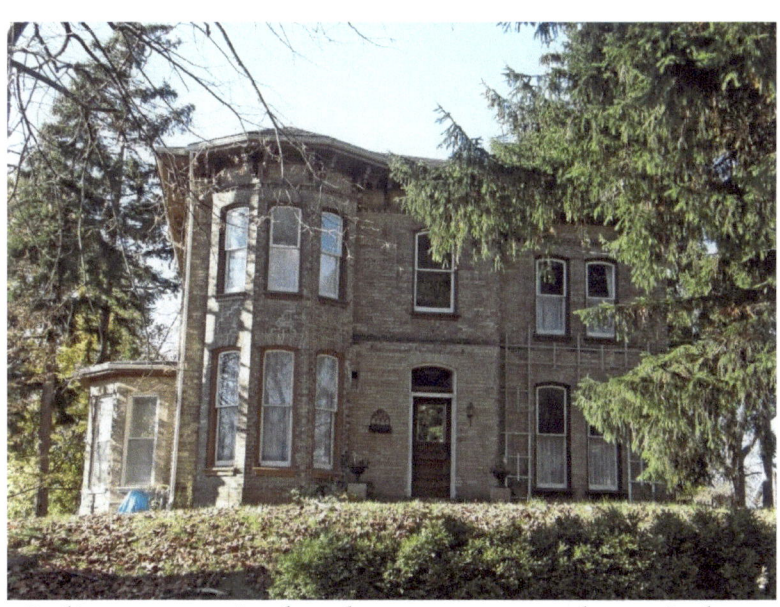

Italianate, cornice brackets, two-storey bay window

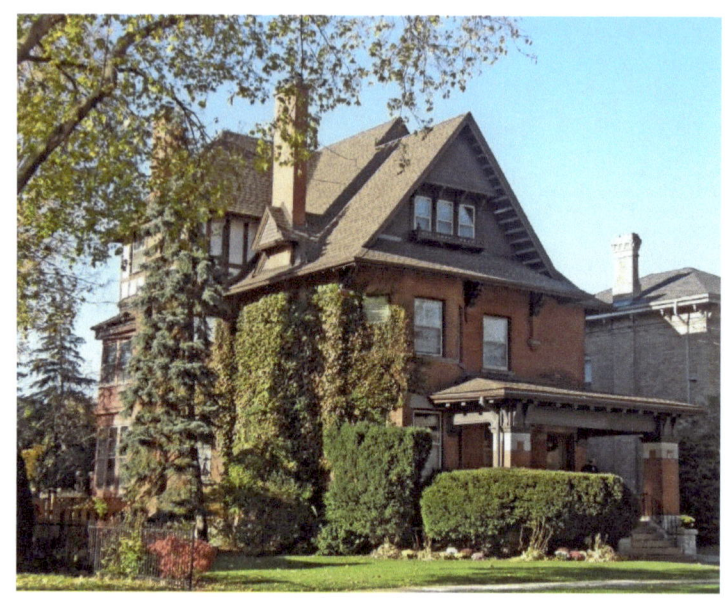

Edwardian

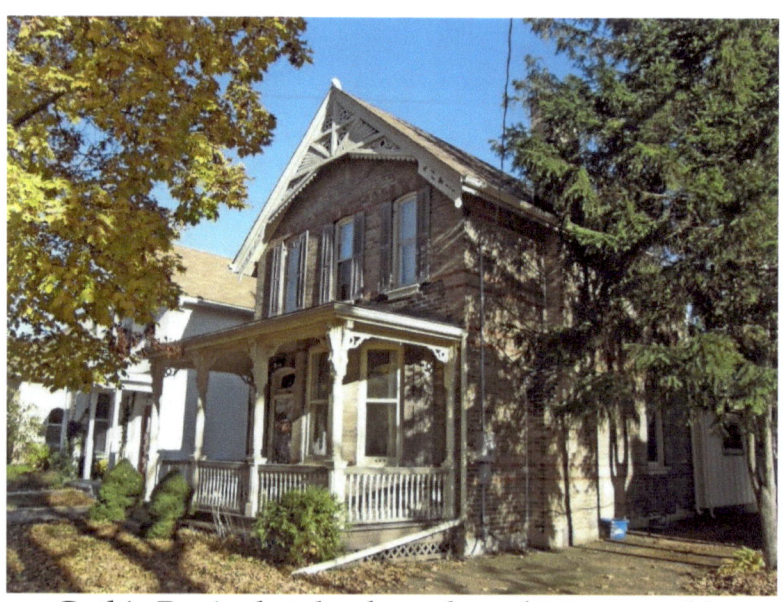

Gothic Revival style - bargeboard trim on gable

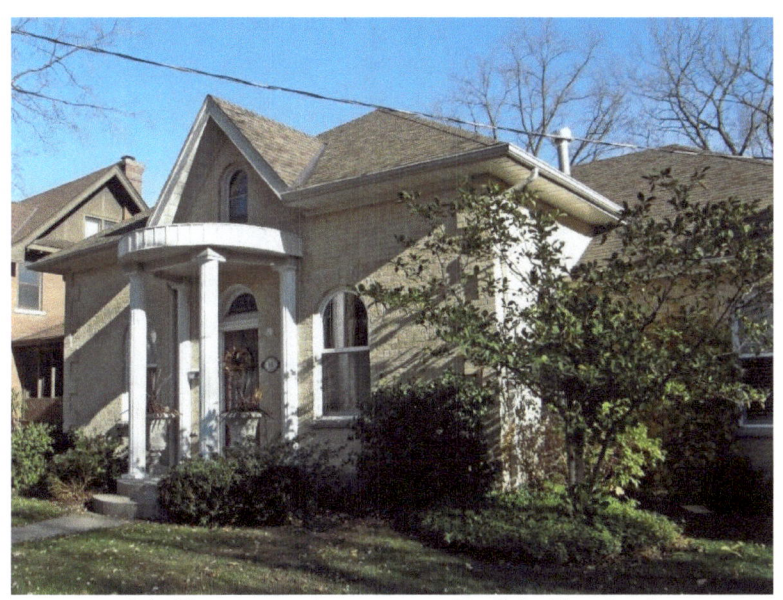

14 Chestnut Avenue – Gothic Revival

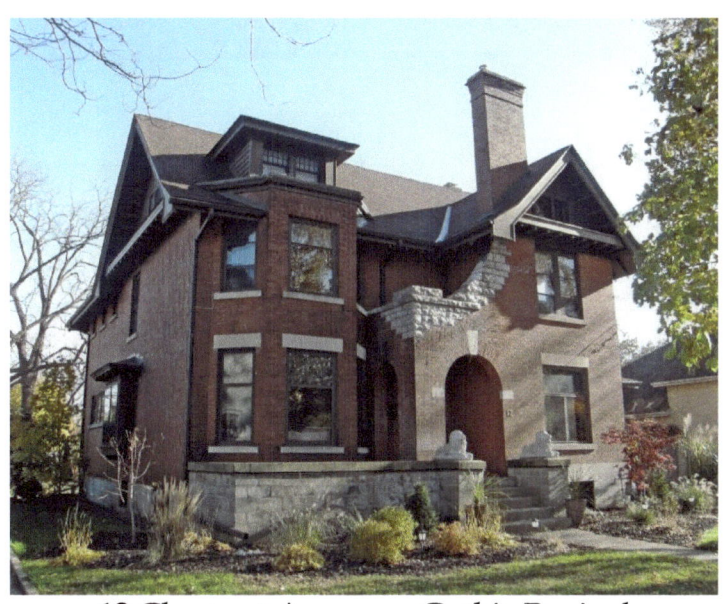

12 Chestnut Avenue – Gothic Revival

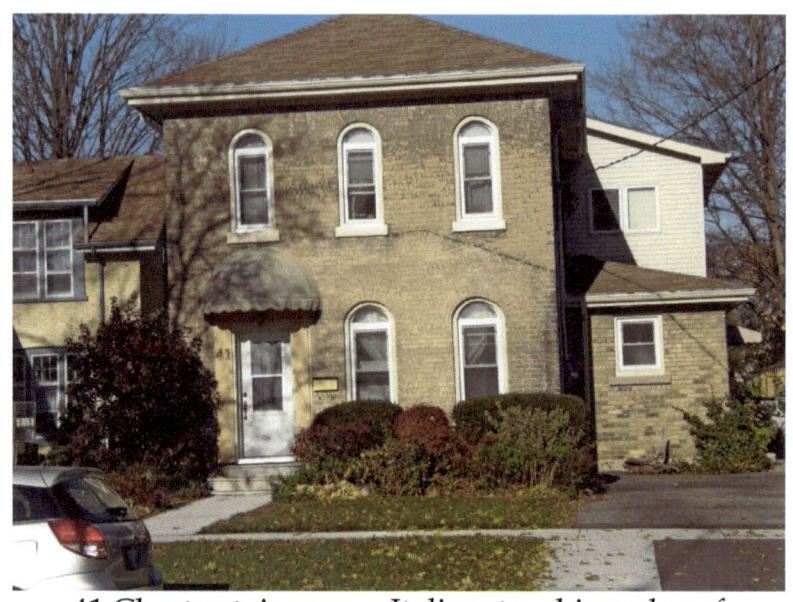

41 Chestnut Avenue - Italianate – hipped roof

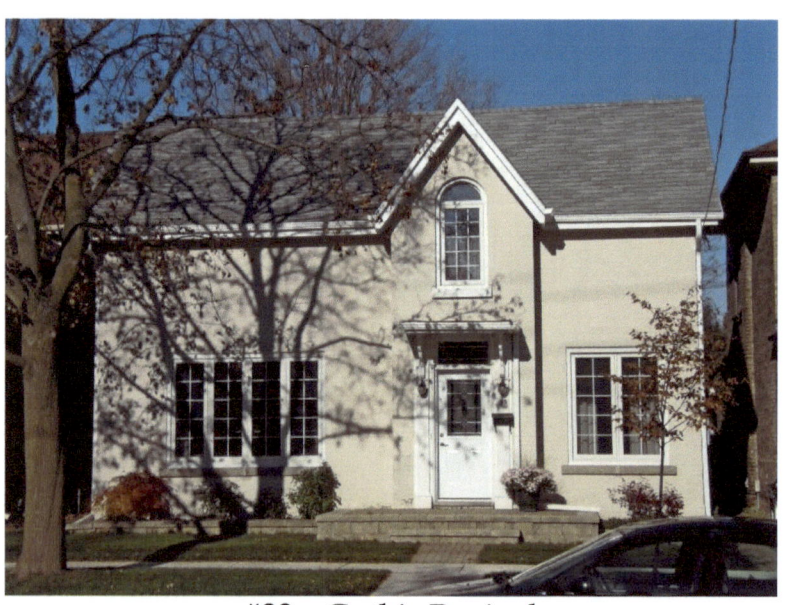

#33 – Gothic Revival

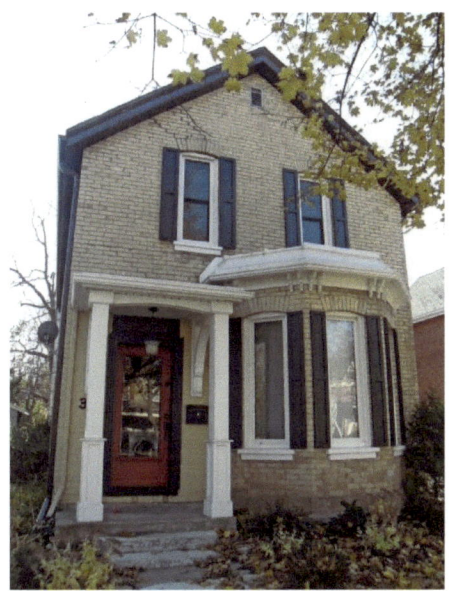

Gothic Revival – bay window

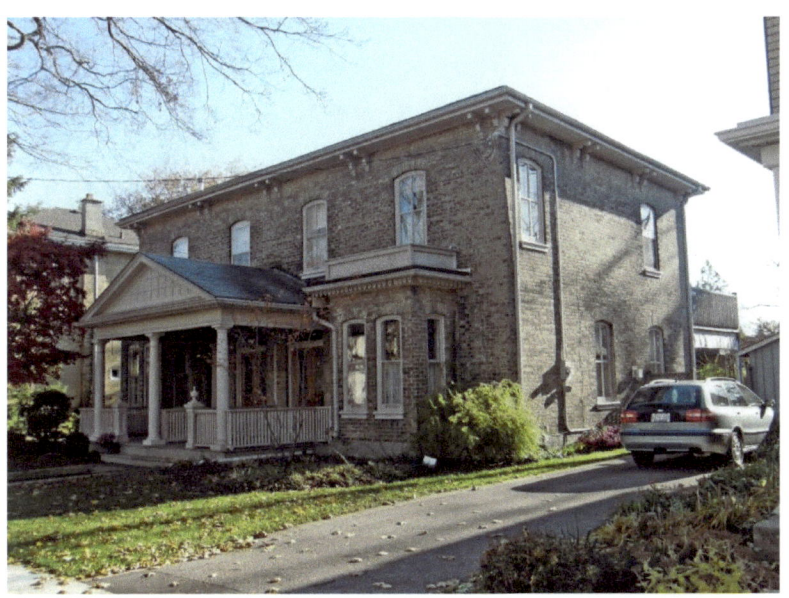

Italianate, rectangular bay window, pediment

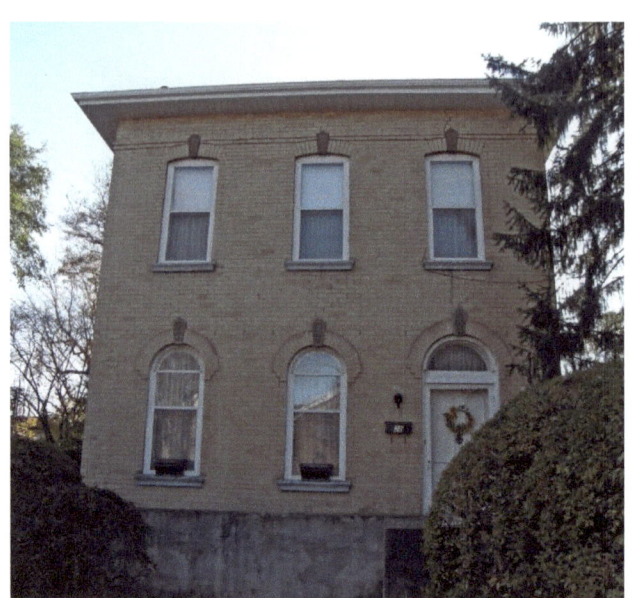

Italianate - keystones

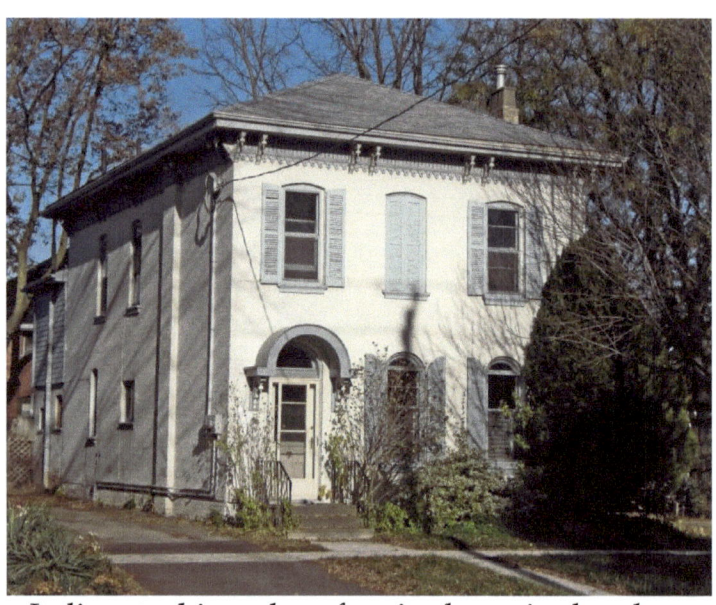

Italianate, hipped roof, paired cornice brackets

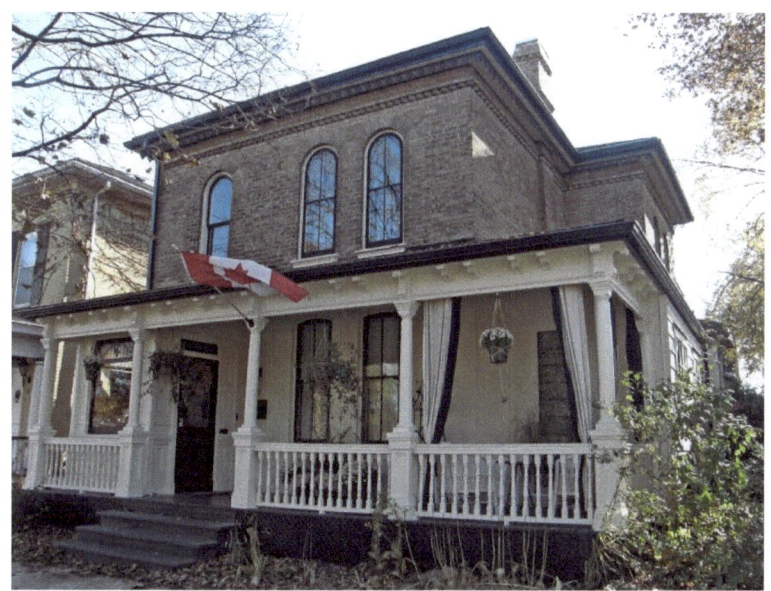

Italianate - dentil detailing in the brickwork
above the upper windows

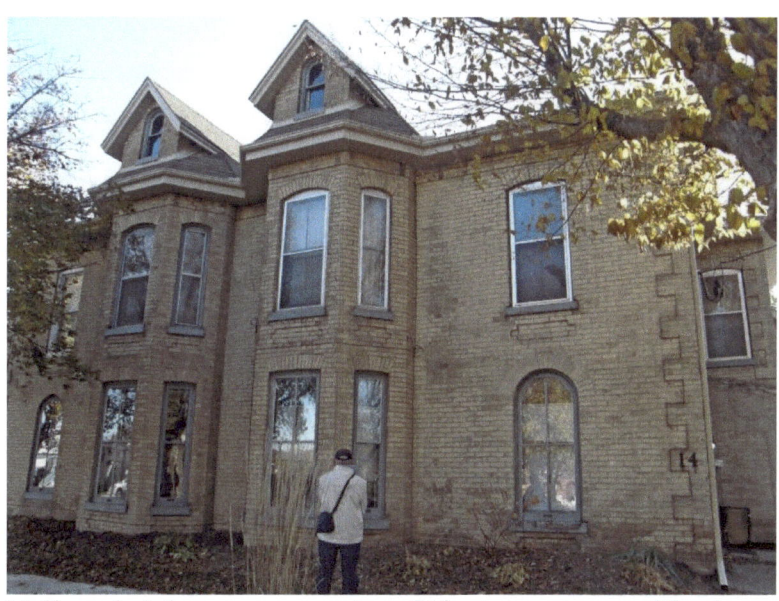

Yellow brick, corner quoins, 2½-storey tower-like bays

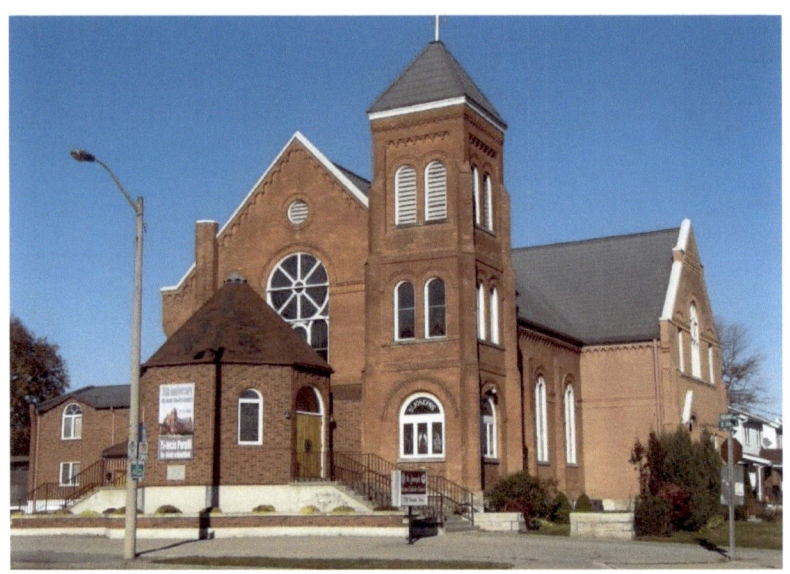

235 Brant Avenue - St. Joseph Roman Catholic Church,
rose window, corbelled dentils

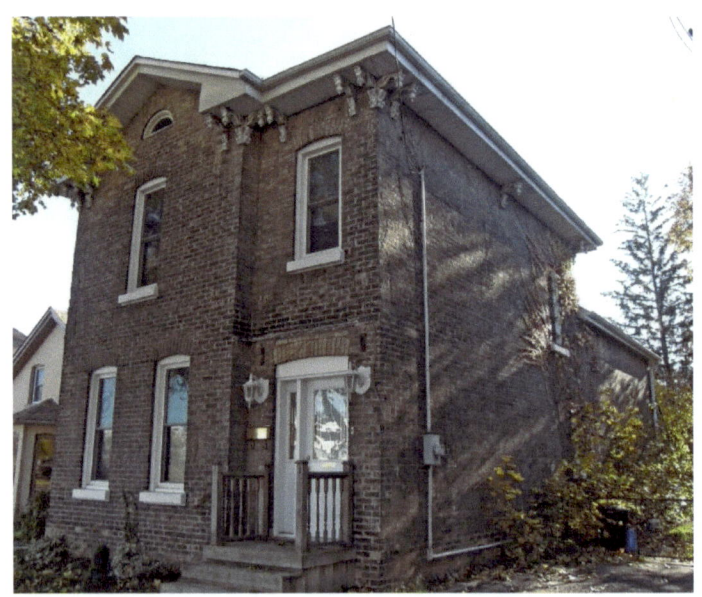

Italianate - paired cornice brackets under the eaves

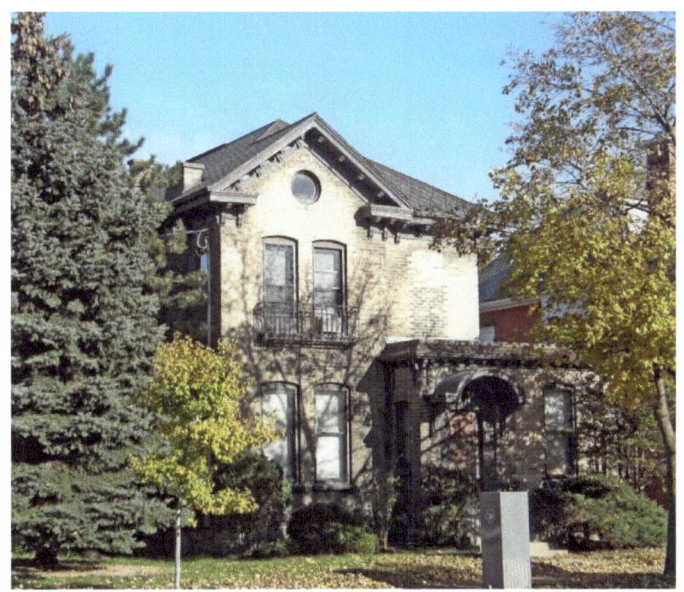

Gothic Revival - cornice return and cornice brackets

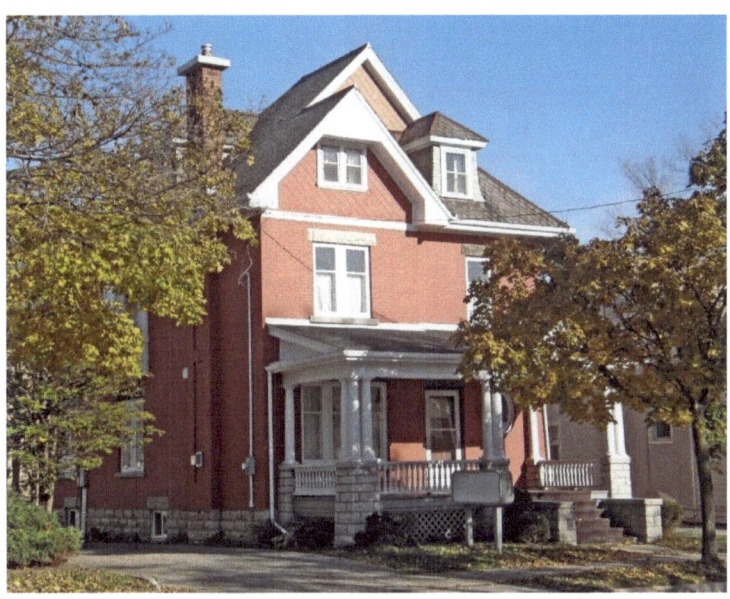

dormer

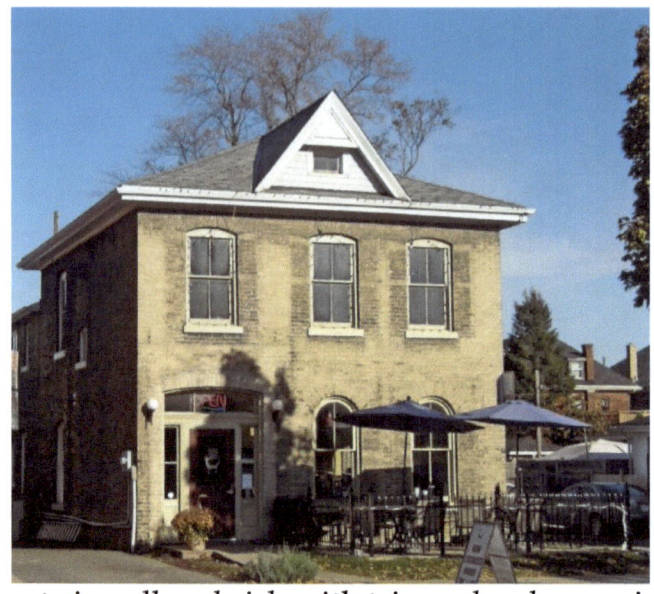

Italianate in yellow brick with triangular dormer in attic

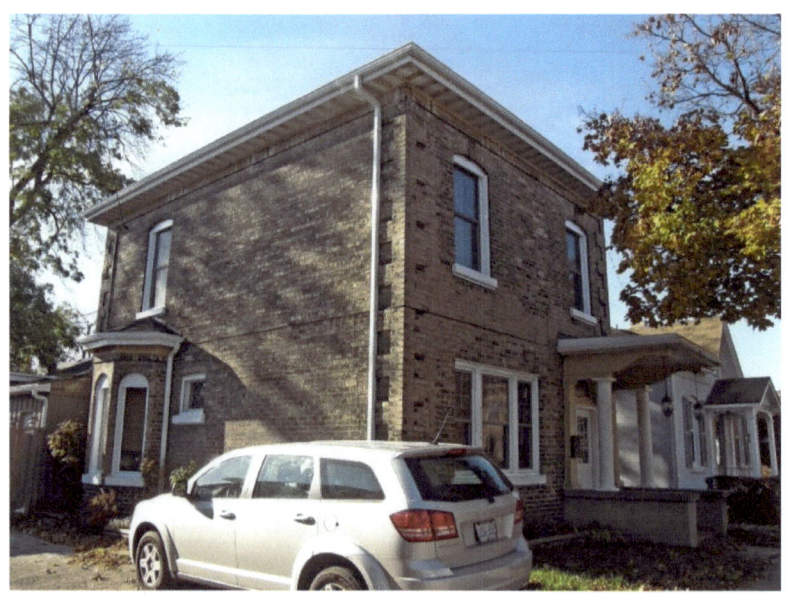

Italianate – yellow brick, corner quoins

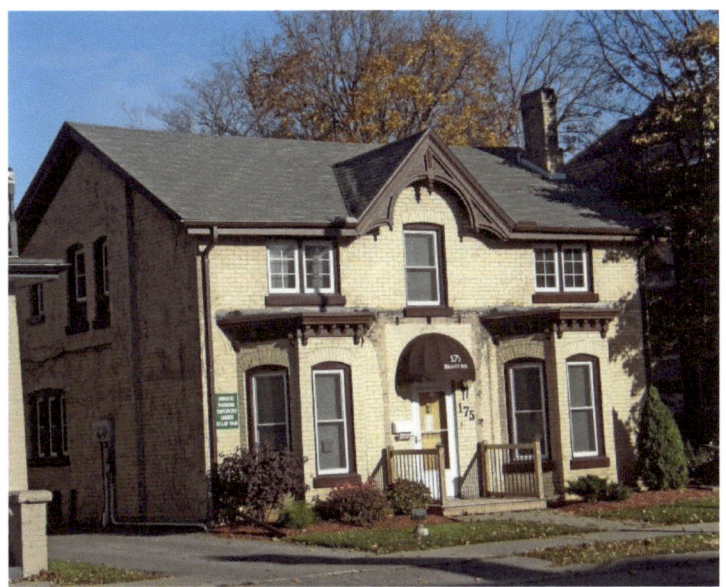

#175 – Gothic Revival, verge board trim on gable,
first floor bay windows

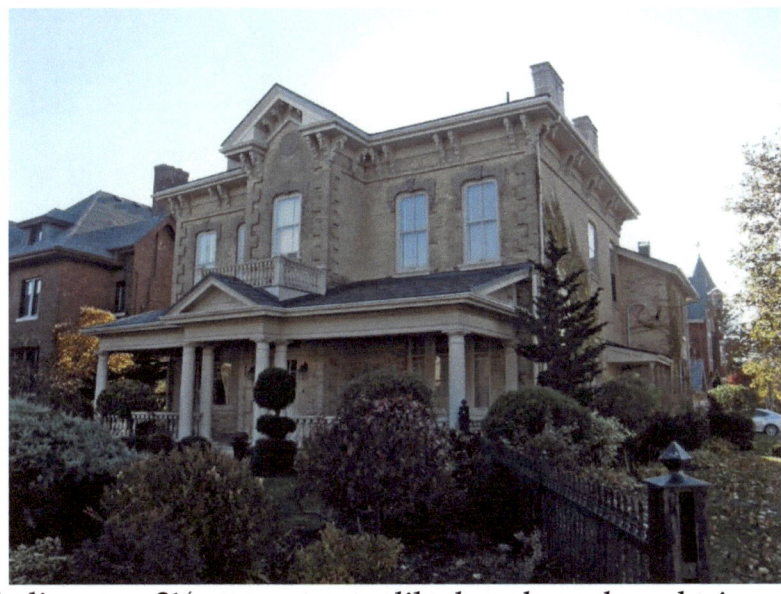

Italianate – 2½ storey tower-like bay, bargeboard trim on
gable with cornice return, paired cornice brackets, pediment

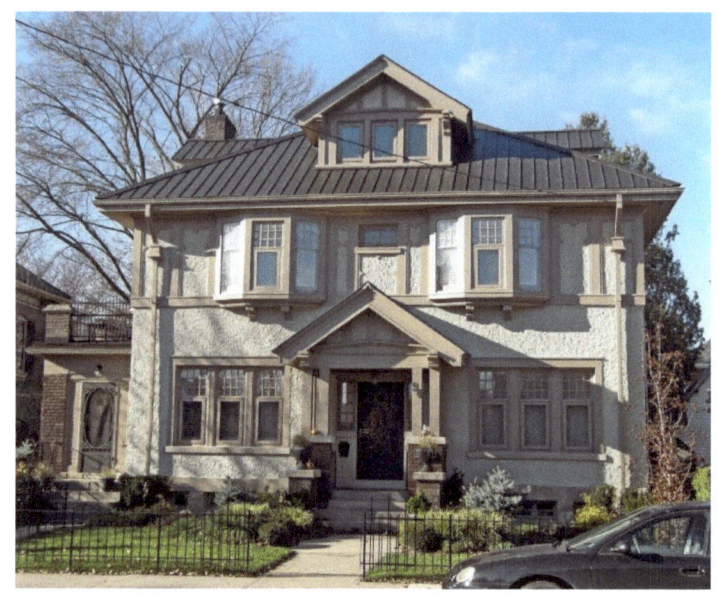

#94 – circa 1914 – Tudor, dormer

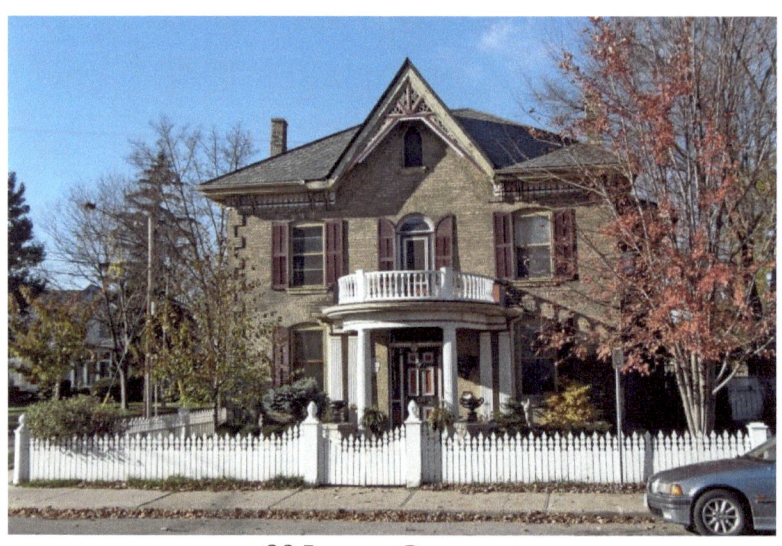

90 Lorne Crescent
Gingerbread trim on Gothic Revival style gable,
balcony on second level

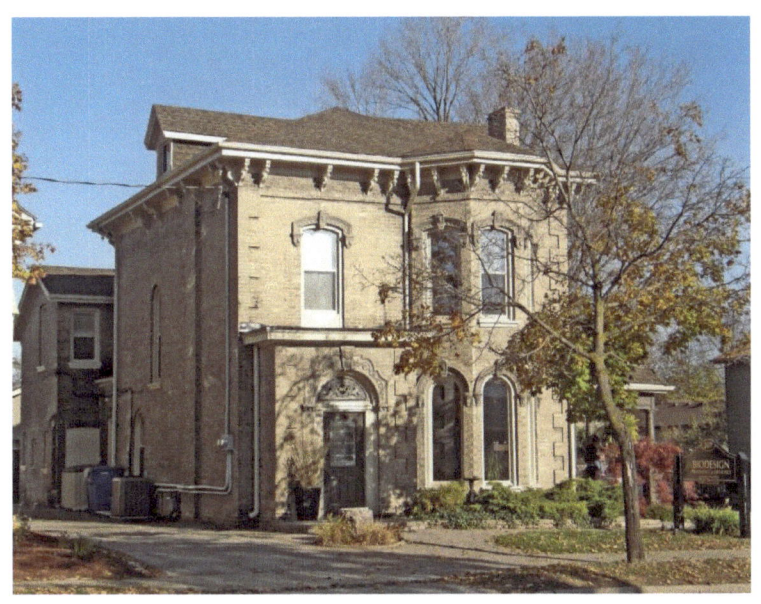

#207 - Italianate – yellow brick, single cornice brackets, corner quoins

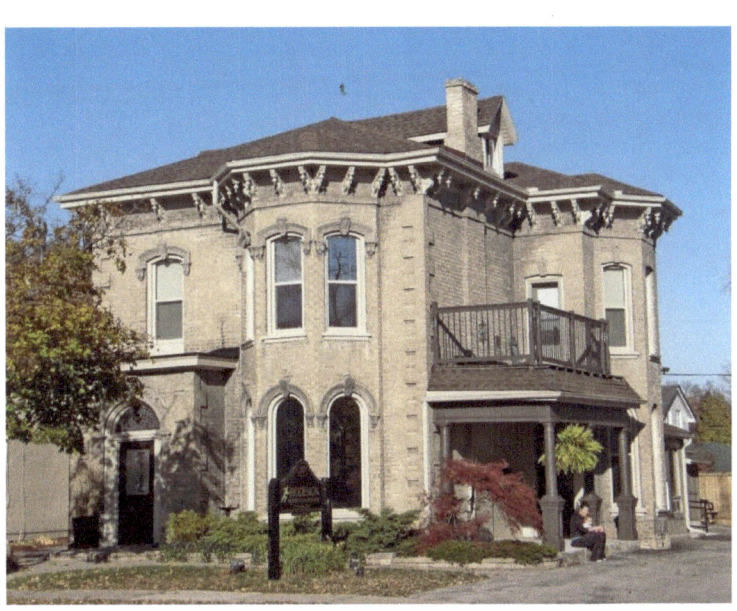

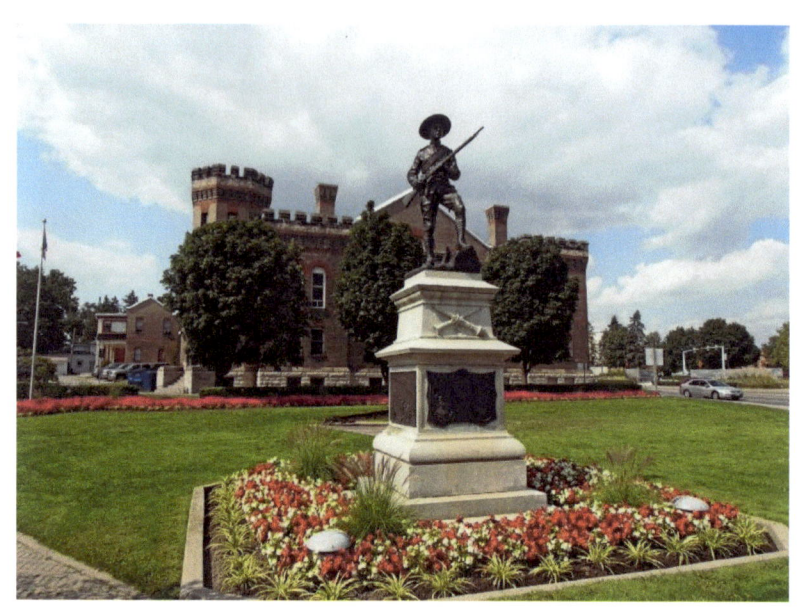

Dufferin Rifles Armoury 1893

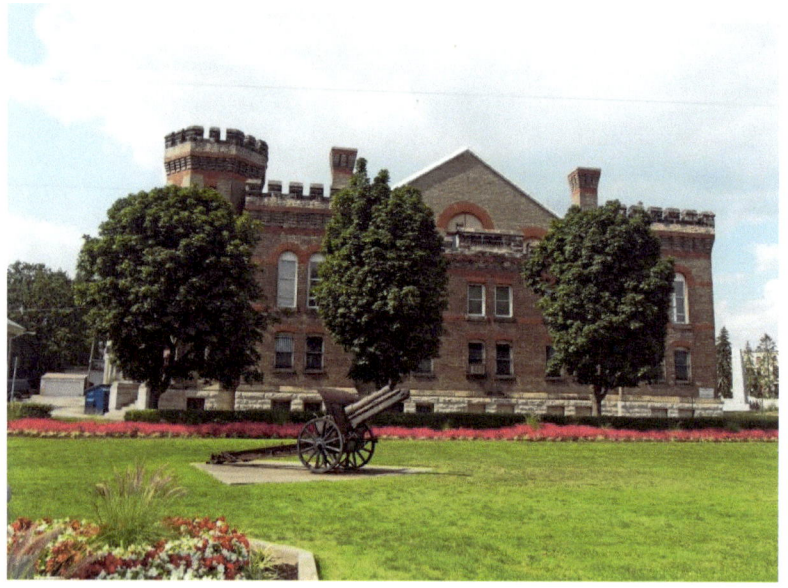

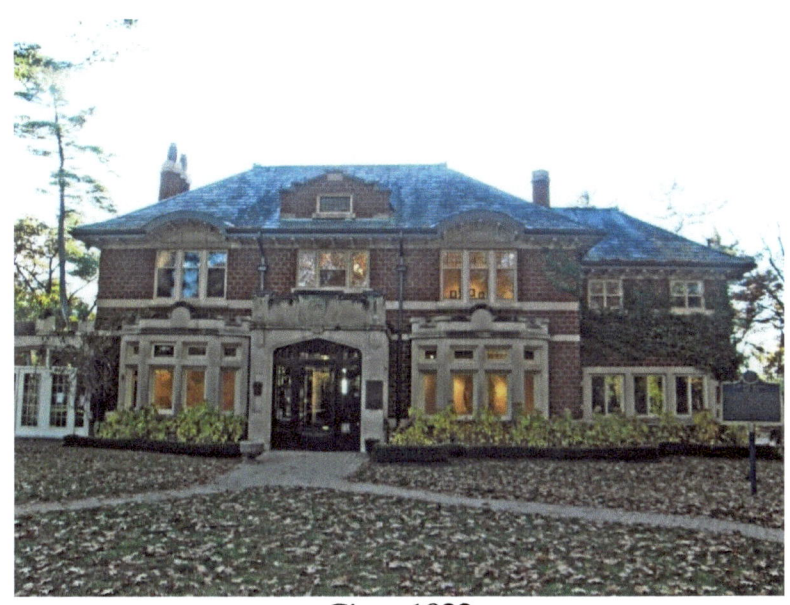

Circa 1922

Glenhyrst Art Gallery of Brantford and Glenhyrst Gardens which overlook the Grand River

Born into a prominent Brantford family, Lawren Harris (1885-1970) began to paint as a child. At the University of Toronto, a professor noticed he sketched during lectures and advised he be sent to Europe to study art. In 1920, he helped found the Group of Seven, an association of landscape artists dedicated to creating a distinctly Canadian form of art. In the 1930s, he became an abstract artist. Harris landscapes such as "North Shore, Lake Superior," and "Icebergs, Davis Strait" remain celebrated Canadian images.

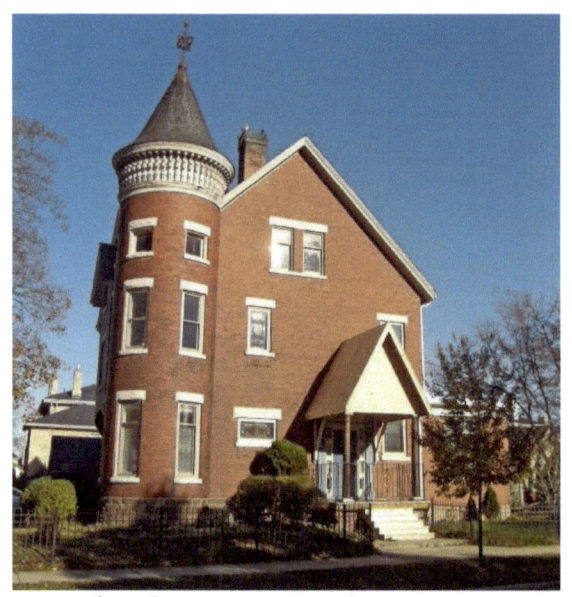

Queen Anne style - 3 storey round turret room with cupola

Shakespeare

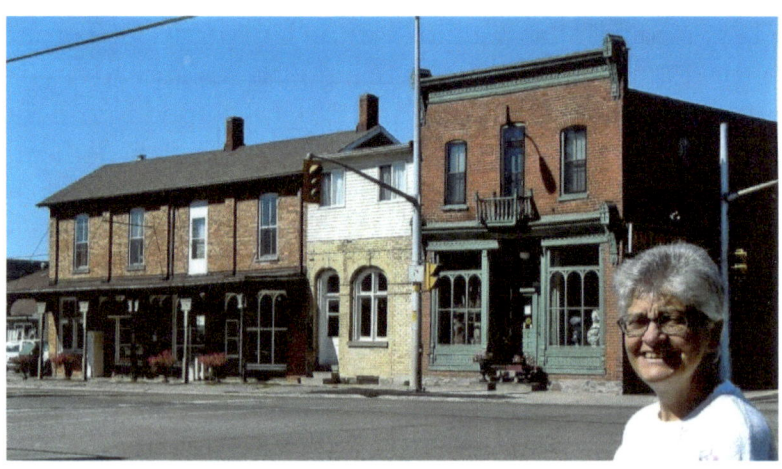

Bethel Road

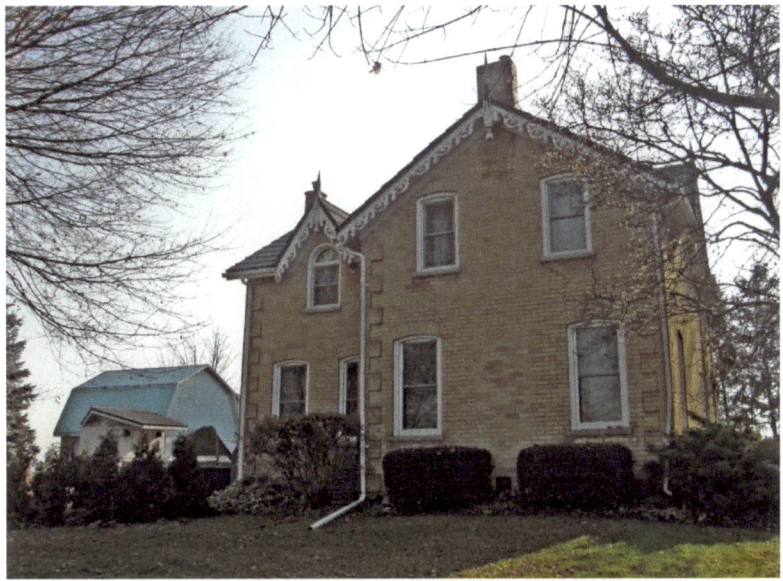

Gothic Revival - verge board with finials

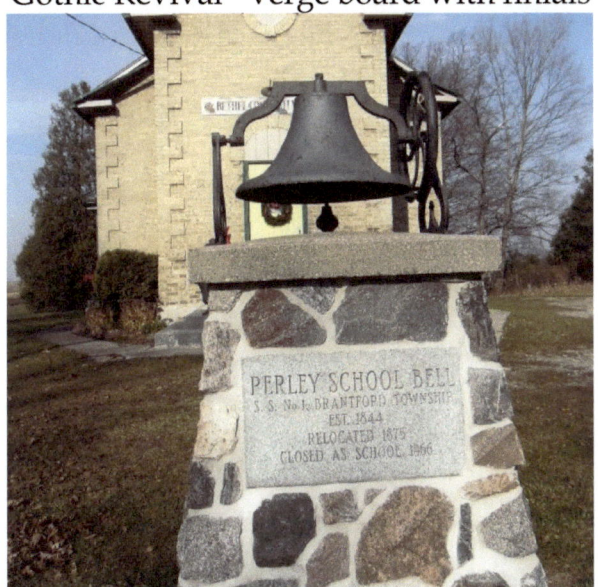

Perley School Bell, S.S. No. 1 Brantford Township,
established 1844, relocated 1875, closed as a school 1966

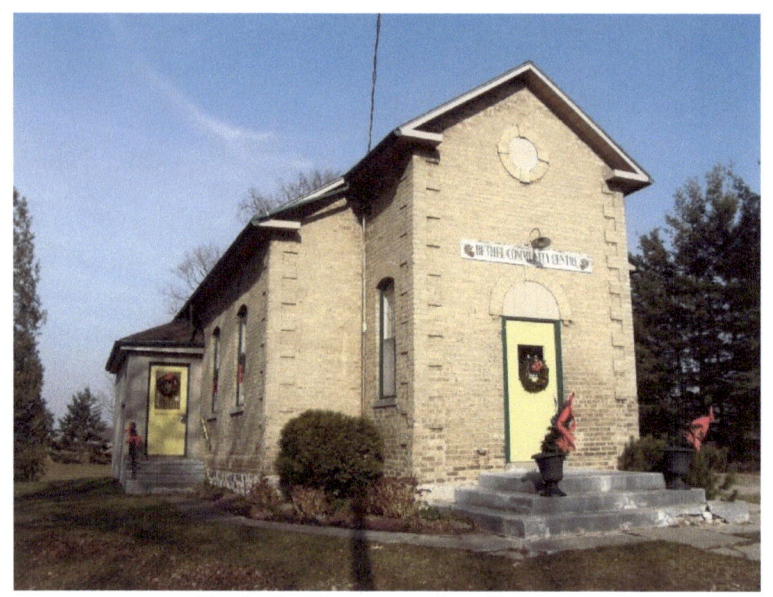

Bethel Community Centre
Cornice return on the gable, corner quoins

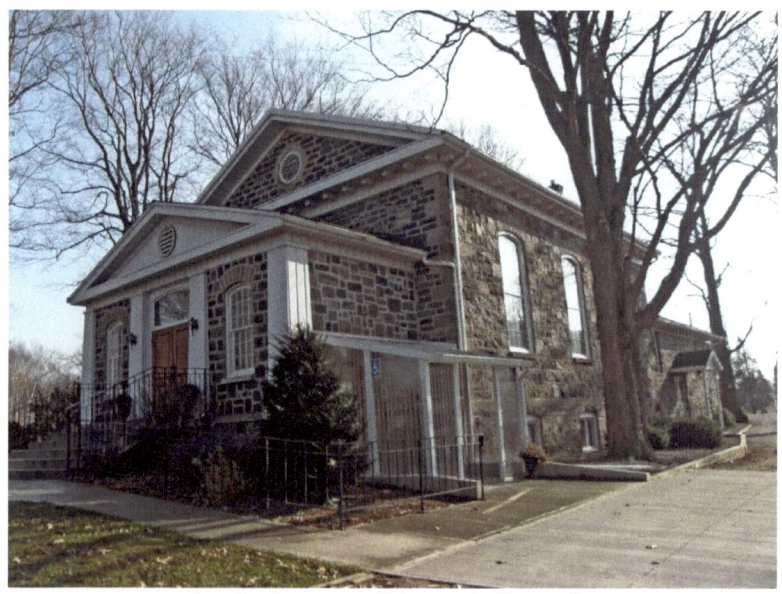

Bethel Stone United Church

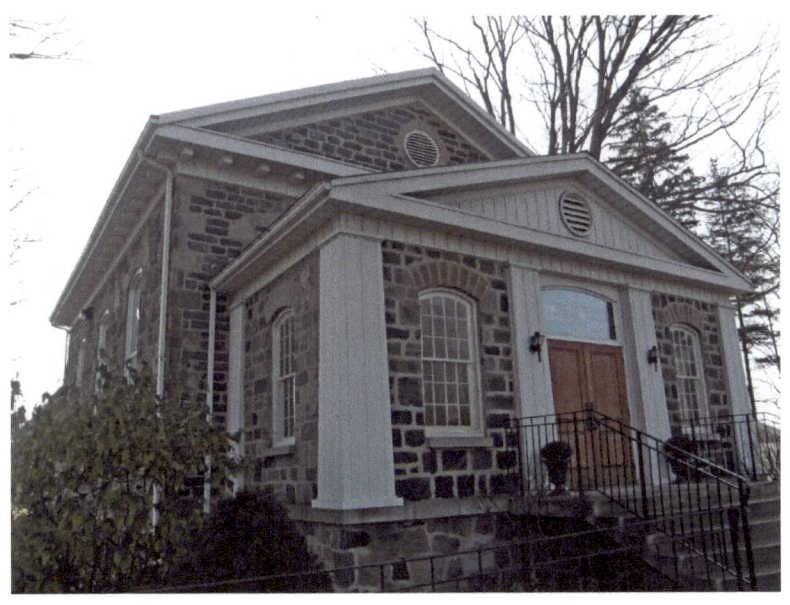

Bethel Stone United Church, 154 Bethel Road
(Methodist Church A.D. 1881)

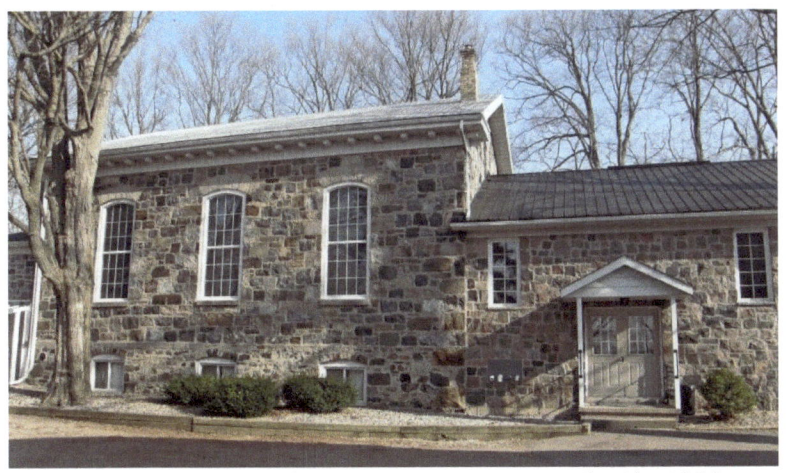

Cobblestone architecture - extension built 1983

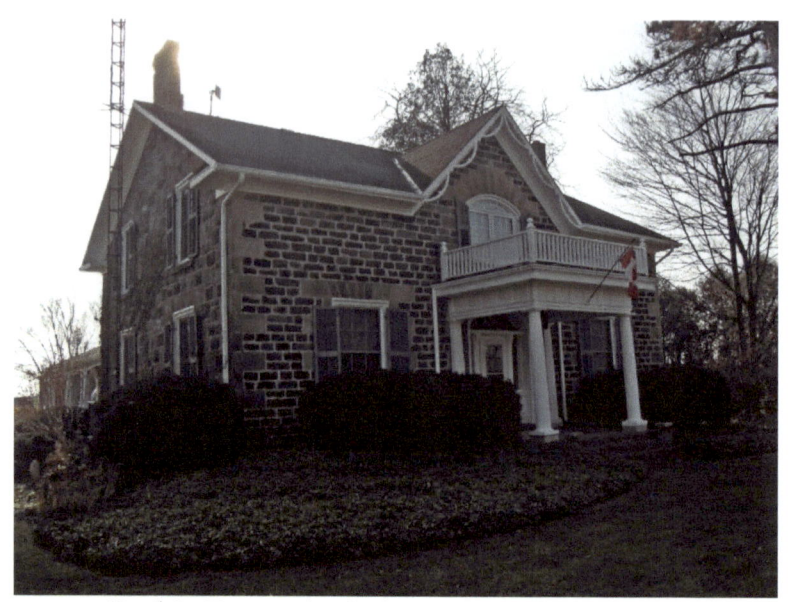

Gothic Revival – balcony on second floor

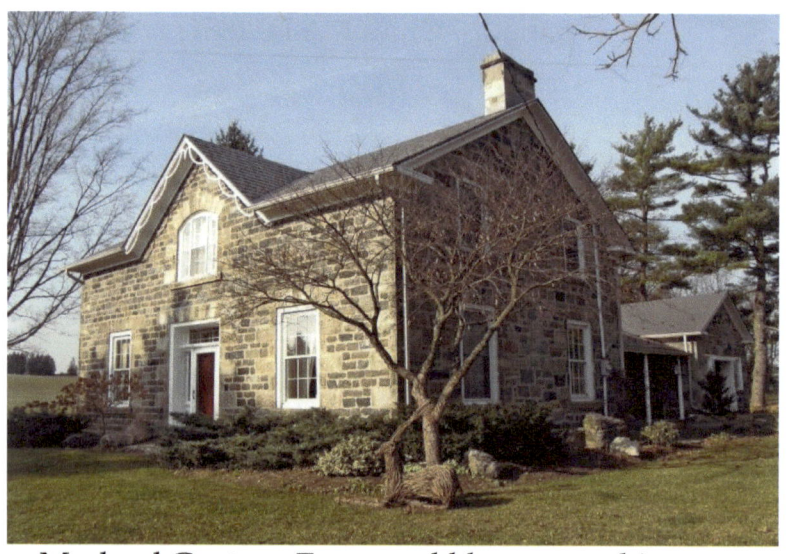

Macland Century Farm - cobblestone architecture

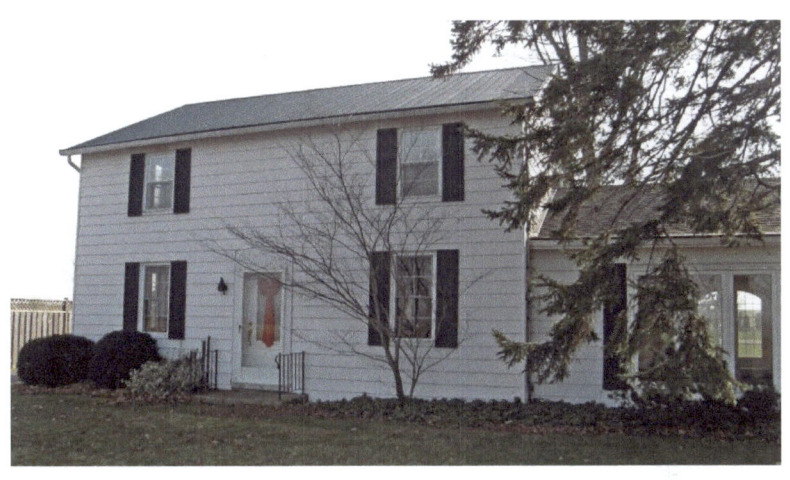

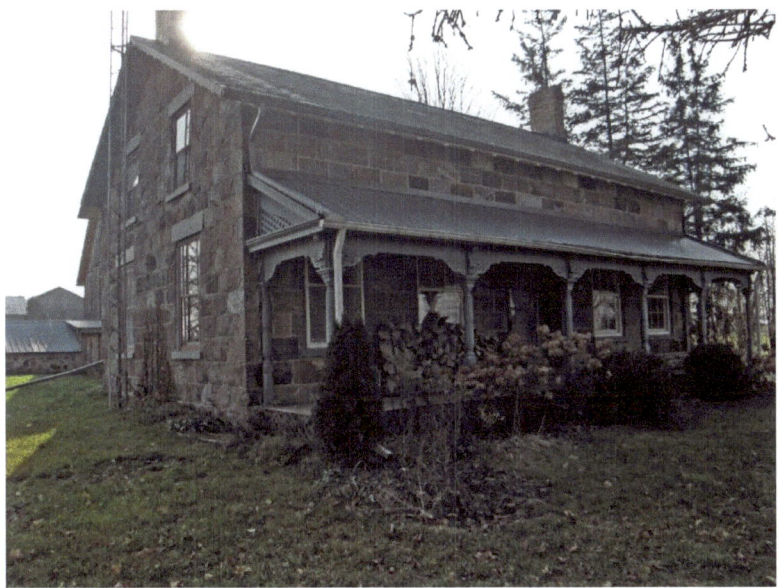

Gothic Revival - cobblestone architecture

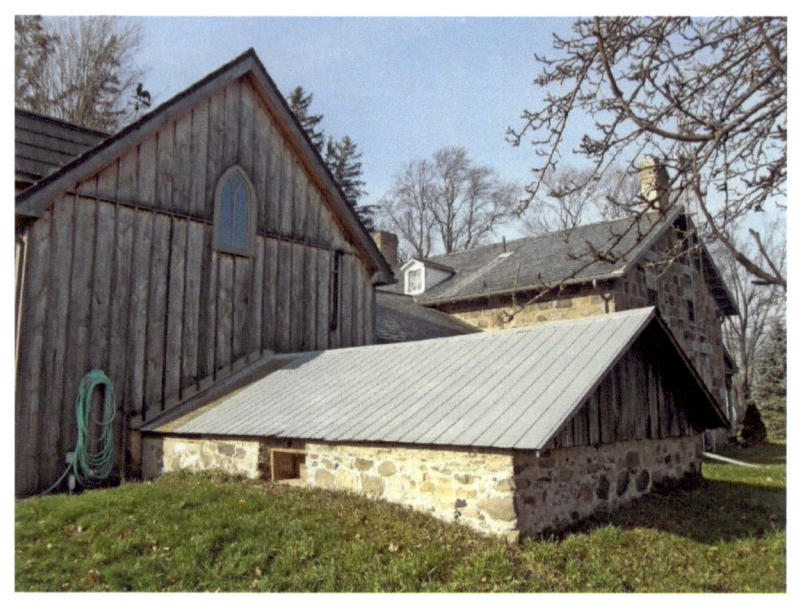

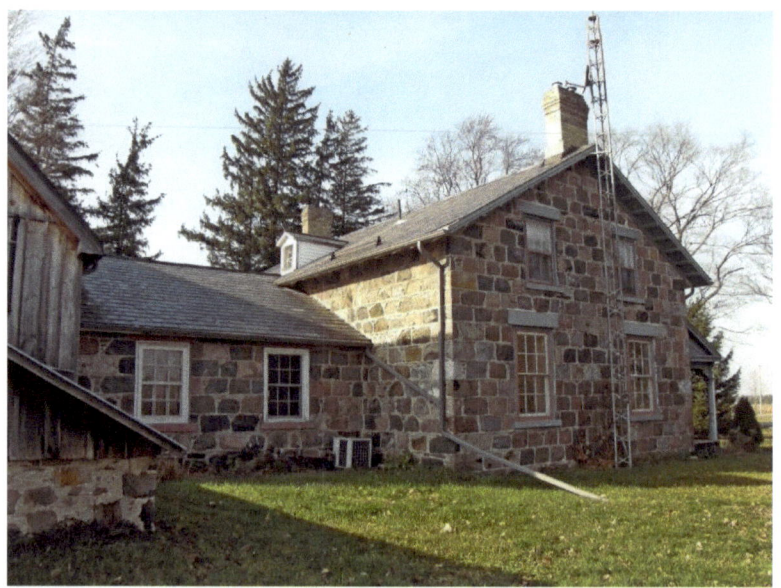

Cobblestone architecture

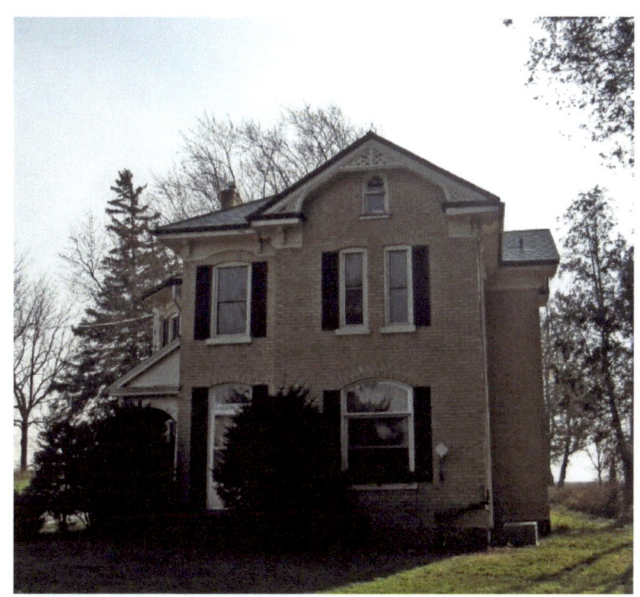

Gothic Revival – verge board trim on gable

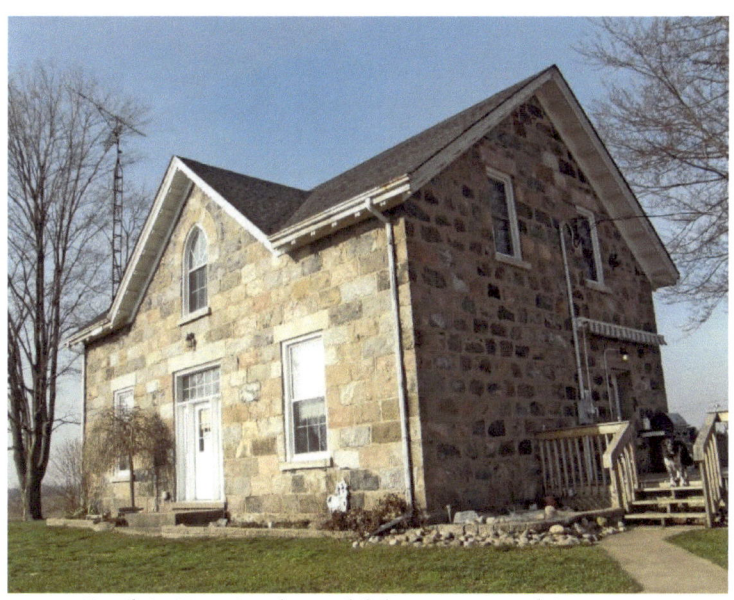

Gothic Revival - cobblestone architecture

Falkland

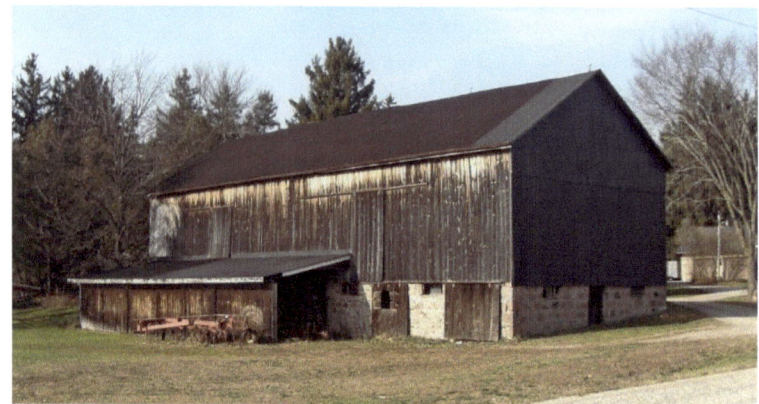

Old barn

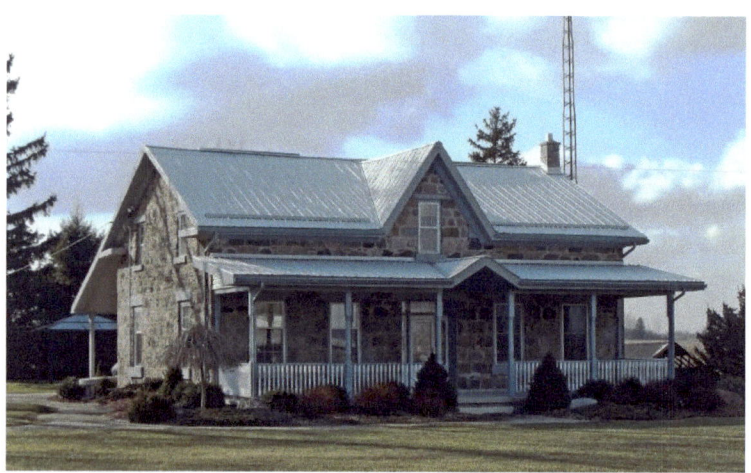

Gothic Revival - cobblestone architecture

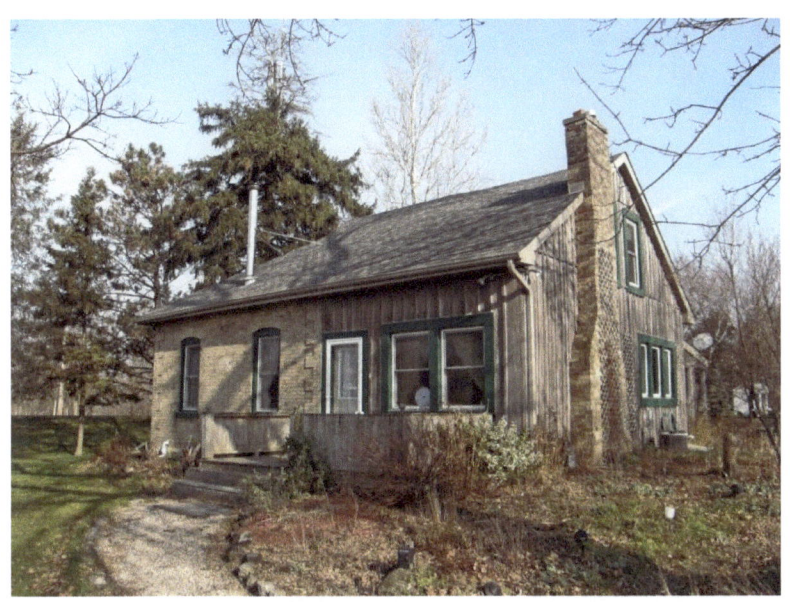

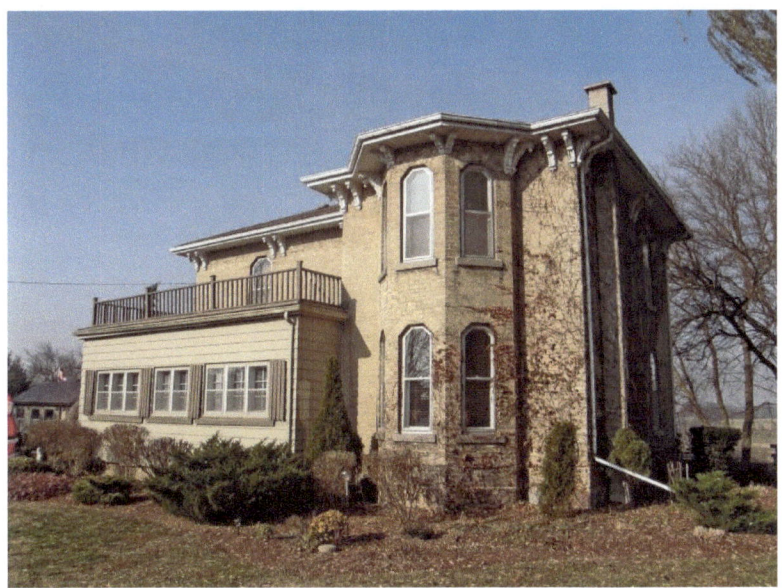

Italianate - paired cornice brackets, yellow brick

Eastwood

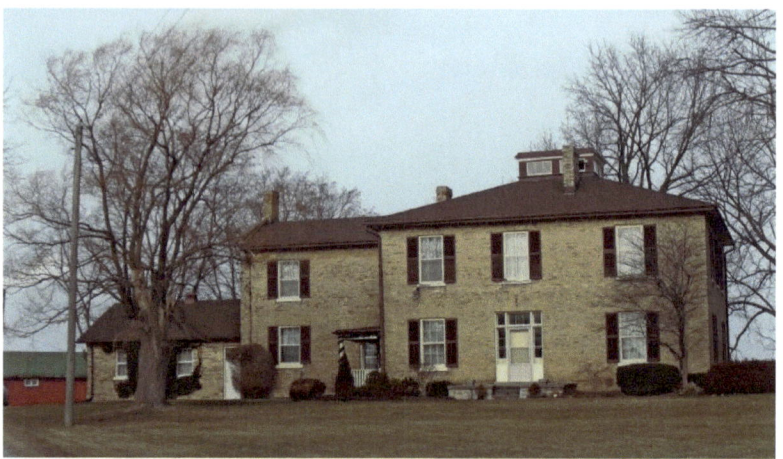

Italianate – hipped roof, belvedere

Etonia

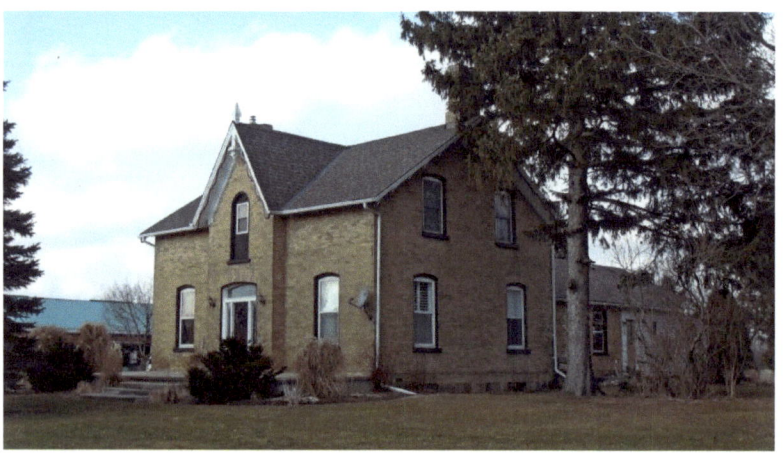

Gothic Revival - finial on the verge board on gable

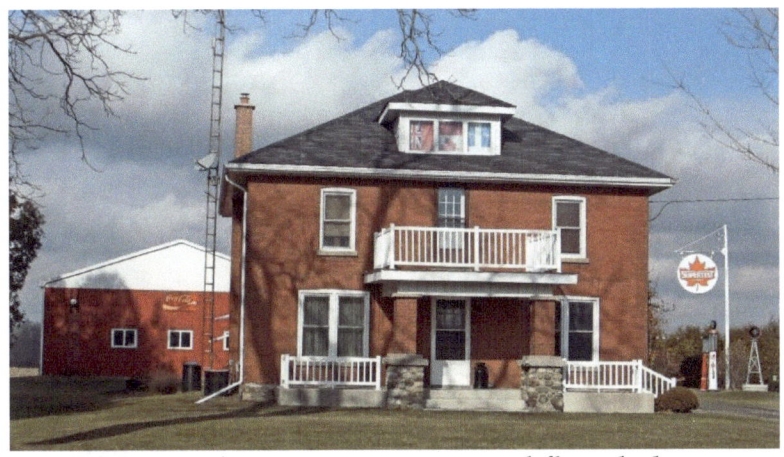

Italianate, dormer in attic, second floor balcony

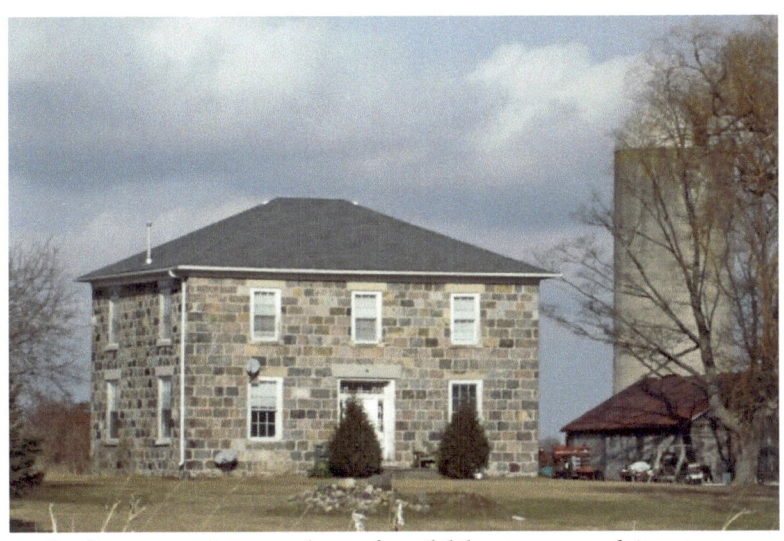

Italianate – hipped roof, cobblestone architecture

Architectural Terms

Banding: Different materials, colours or textures used in horizontal bands along a wall. Example: see Page 31	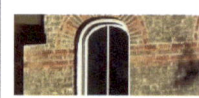
Belvedere: (from the Italian "beautiful view") an architectural feature on a roof, in a garden or on a terrace that gives a beautiful view. Example: Eastwood (see Page 64)	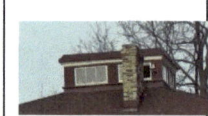
Brackets: a decorative or weight-bearing structural element which forms a right angle with one side against a wall and the other under a projecting surface such as an eave or roof. Example: see Page 29	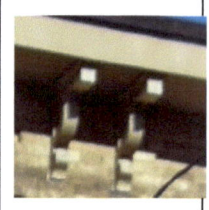
Buttress: a masonry structure built against or projecting from a wall which serves to support or reinforce the wall. In Canadian architecture, they are sometimes used for decoration. Example: see Page 10	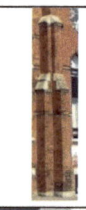
Capital: The uppermost finish or decoration on a column. An Ionic column has a small base, a thin elegant shaft, and a capital composed of volutes which are carved whirls or twists that take the form of a scroll. A Corinthian column is characterized by a rounded capital decorated with acanthus leaves and a square abacus (the uppermost portion of a capital directly below the entablature) on tall slender columns. Example: Ionic – see Page 10 Corinthian – see Page 12	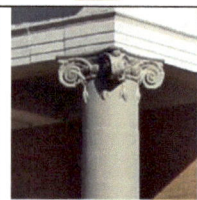 Ionic 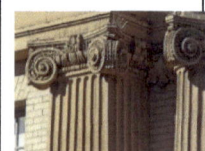 Corinthian

Cobblestone architecture: Refers to the use of cobblestones embedded in mortar as a method for erecting walls on houses and commercial buildings. Example: see Page 61	
Cornice: originally the wooden overhang of the roof. With the use of stone, brick, iron and steel, the cornice is any projecting shelf at the top of a ceiling or roof. They can be very decorative. Example: see Page 50	
Cornice Return: decorative element on the end of a gable. Example: see Page 47	
Cupola: A domed or curved roof rising from a building as a decorative element. Example: see Page 54	
Dentil Moulding: an even series of rectangles used as ornamental decoration in cornices. Example: see Page 15	
Dichromatic brickwork: the use of two colours of brick, tile or slate to decorate a façade. Example: 26 Lorne Crescent (see Page 18)	
Dome: Any roof structure that is curved and spans an ultimately circular base. A squinch is a construction filling in the upper angles of a square room so as to form a base to receive an **octagonal** or **spherical dome**. When a square space is vaulted to provide a circular space for a **dome** the resulting curved triangular supports are called pendentives. This is most common in Byzantine architecture. Example: Laurier Brantford (see Page 10)	

Dormer: (French for "sleep") a gable end window that pierces through the plane of a sloping roof surface to create usable space in the top floor or attic of a building by adding headroom. Example: see Page 27	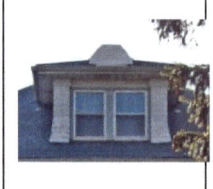
Gable: the triangular portion of a wall between the edges of a sloping roof. Example: see Page 31	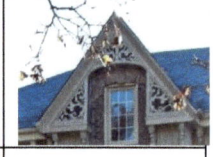
Hipped Roof: a roof where all sides slope downwards to the walls with no gables. Example: 41 Chestnut Avenue (see Page 42)	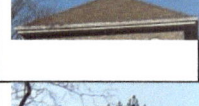
Iron Cresting: A decorative ornament along the top of a roof. Iron cresting was popular in the Baroque era and also in Italianate, Victorian, Second Empire and Queen Anne styles of architecture. Example: see Page 38	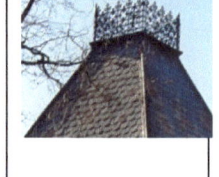
Keystones and Voussoirs: a voussoir is a wedge-shaped element used in building an arch. A keystone is the central stone that locks all the stones into position, allowing the arch to bear weight. A keystone is often enlarged and embellished. Example: see Page 44	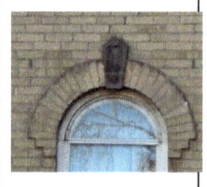
Mansard Roof: This style was popularized by Francois Mansart (1598-1666), an accomplished architect of the French Baroque period and especially fashionable during the Second French Empire (1852-1870). This roof is almost flat on the top section, with two slopes on each of its sides with the lower slope at a steeper angle than the upper and having dormer windows. Example: see Page 9	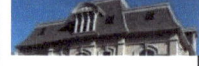

Palladian Window: a large window that is divided into three sections with the centre section larger than the two side sections and usually arched. Example: see Page 25	
Pediment: a triangular section above the horizontal structure (entablature), typically supported by columns. The inside of the triangle is called the tympanum. Example: Bank of Montreal (see Page 11)	
Pilaster: a slightly projecting column built into or applied to the face of a wall for additional structural support. Example: Federal Building (see Page 14)	
Quoin: masonry blocks at the corner of a wall, often a decorative feature, usually larger or of a different colour than the rest of the wall. Example: see Page 45	
Rose Window: a circular window with ornamental tracery radiating from the centre. Example: see Page 10	
Turret: a small tower that projects from the wall of a building. Example: Calvary Baptist Church	
Verge board and Finial: also called bargeboards – hang from the projecting end of a roof and are often elaborately carved and ornamented. **Finial:** ornament added to the top of a gable, pinnacle, canopy or spire – a Gothic element. Examples: Verge board: Bethel Road (see Page 55) Finial: Etonia (see Page 64)	

Edwardian, 1900-1930 – This style bridges the ornate and elaborate styles of the Victorian era and the simplified styles of the 20th century. Balanced facades, simple roof lines, dormer windows, large front porches, and smooth brick surfaces are its characteristics. Example: see Page 25	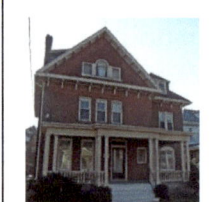
Gothic Revival, 1830-1890 – These decorative buildings have sharply-pitched gables with highly detailed verge boards, pointed-arch window openings, and dichromatic brickwork. It is a common style in Ontario. Example: see Page 19	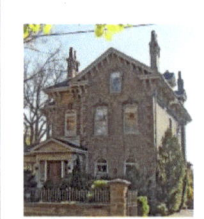
Italianate, 1850-1900 – It has wide-bracketed eaves, belvederes, wrap-around verandahs. Example: see Page 29	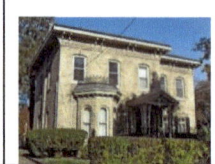
Queen Anne, 1885-1900 – This style is distinguished by an irregular outline featuring a combination of an offset tower, broad gables, projecting two-storey bays, verandahs, multi-sloped roofs, and tall, decorative chimneys. A mixture of brick and wood is common. Windows often have one large single-paned bottom sash and small panes in the upper sash. Example: see Page 28	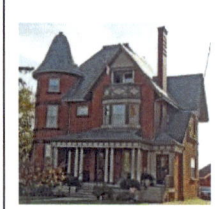

Second Empire, 1860-1880 – The mansard roof is the most noteworthy feature of this style and is evidence of the French origins. Projecting central towers and one or two-storey bays can also be present. Example: see Page 9	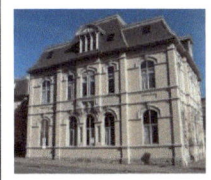
Tudor Revival – exposed timbers with stucco infill, multi-paned windows. Example: see Page 50	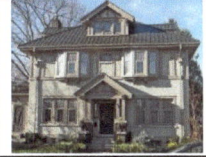